THE WATTS HISTORY OF SPORTS

the super bowl

MARK STEWART

Researched and Edited by

MIKE KENNEDY

FRANKLIN WATTS
A Division of Scholastic Inc.
New York • Toronto • London • Auckland • Sydney
Mexico City • New Delhi • Hong Kong
Danbury, Connecticut

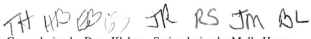

Cover design by Dave Klaboe   Series design by Molly Heron

Cover photo/frontispiece IDs: (center left) Pittsburgh Steelers' quarterback Terry Brad-
shaw in 1979 during Super Bowl XIII; (center right) Vince Lombardi Trophy; (clockwise
from upper left) kicker for the Miami Dolphins; Joe Namath; San Francisco 49ers Joe
Montana (16) and Guy McIntyre (62) celebrating a touchdown in Super Bowl XXIV;
Dallas Cowboys Deion Sanders and Pittsburgh Steelers Willy Williams (27) during Super
Bowl XXX in Tempe, Arizona; Raymond James Stadium in Tampa, Florida; Green Bay
Packers coach Vince Lombardi celebrating his team's victory in Super Bowl I in 1967.

Photographs © 2002: AP/Wide World Photos: 120 (Elise Amendola), 87 (Al Behrman)
127 (Rick Bowmer), cover bottom right (Hans Deryk), cover top right (Mark Duncan),
105 (Bob Galbraith), 100, 128 (John Gaps III), 4 (Olivia Hanley), 64, 93, 99 (Rusty
Kennedy), 71 (Bill Kostroun), 102 (Wilfredo Lee), cover center right (Dave Martin), 106,
115 (Doug Mills), 103 (Douglas C. Pizac) 121, 131 (Ed Reinke), 109 (Eric Risberg), 78,
81, 112, 116, 123 (Amy Sancetta), 42, 77, 90 (Phil Sandlin), 79 (Reed Saxon), 97 (Olga
Shalygin), cover center left, cover top, 6, 16, 18, 24, 25, 29, 30, 34, 35, 37, 39, 40, 46, 47,
48, 49, 51, 52, 58, 62, 67, 68; Corbis Images: 134 (AFP), cover bottom left, 11, 28, 60,
72, 73 (Bettmann), cover bottom (Duomo), 5 (Jeff Haynes/AFP), cover top left (Wally
McNamee), 94 (Bruno Torres/Bettmann), 98 (David Tulis/Bettmann), 57, 83 (Glenn
Wagner/Bettmann), 130 (Rhona Wise/AFP), 31; Team Stewart, Inc.: 8 (Complete Sports
Publications), 14 (The Grow Ahead Press), 7 (National Football League), 132 (The New
York Daily News), 17 (Sports Underwriters), 53, 74 left, 74 right (The Topps Company),
84 (The Upper Deck Company).

Library of Congress Cataloging-in-Publication Data

Stewart, Mark.
    The Super Bowl / Mark Stewart.
    p. cm. — (The Watts history of sports)
    Includes bibliographical references and index.
    Summary: A game-by-game account of the thirty-six Super Bowls
    that have been played from its first competition in 1967 through
    the game played in January 2001.
    ISBN 0-531-11952-1 (lib. bdg.)
    1. Super Bowl—History—Juvenile literature. [1. Super Bowl—History.
    2. Football—History.] 1. Title. II. Series.
    GV956.2.S8 S76 2002
    796.332'648'09—dc21   2001005726

CONTENTS

The Super Bowl has become North America's most-watched sporting event. As the New England Patriots learned after upsetting the Rams in 2002, the team that wins the game can expect a heroes' welcome.

INTRODUCTION

Every sport likes to boast that its championship game is the ultimate game. Each offers its fans something different and special, something that sets it apart from all the others. Soccer's World Cup has 90 minutes of continuous action and strategy. Hockey's Stanley Cup can be decided by a fraction of an inch, in the blink of an eye. Baseball's World Series can come down to one pitch, basketball's NBA Finals to one shot. Yet for fans who like their action and drama crammed into one 60-minute, winner-take-all contest, nothing compares to professional football's Super Bowl.

The moment one Super Bowl ends, the buildup begins for the next one. Players begin focusing on the season ahead; teams start preparing for the college draft; coaches analyze their players' strengths and weaknesses; and fans evaluate their team's chances of getting to the big game. One of the most exciting things about the Super Bowl is that, because the National Football League schedule is only 16 games long, every team has a chance of making it there. A good draft, smart coaching, a few lucky bounces, and a handful of star players are all it takes to advance to the playoffs. It is not unusual for a team to finish last in its division one year, only to challenge for the top spot the next. And once you make it to the NFL's postseason, anything can happen.

While the teams battle it out to see who gets to play in the Super Bowl, officials in the city hosting football's premier event are busy working out a million different details in order to make everything go smoothly. It is not just the game they are concerned about. The week leading up to the Super Bowl features huge parties, important business gatherings, and a not-so-small army of newspaper, magazine, television, radio, and online journalists all looking for an inside scoop, a great human-interest story, or an exclusive interview. Add to that 50,000 or so fans flooding into the city a day or two before game kickoff, and it is no wonder that the NFL changes locations for the Super Bowl each year. The city needs a year or two just to recover!

John Elway (#7) of the Denver Broncos answers questions during a pregame media event. The crush of reporters is just one of the distractions faced by players and coaches in the days leading up to the Super Bowl.

The first Super Bowl was held in 1967. This makes it the youngest of the major team-sports championships. Could the game have been held earlier? Not really. A lot of powerful forces had to come together to make such an event possible—and these forces were not in place until the mid-1960s.

Prior to the 1960s, professional football was not nearly as popular as it is today. Most fans preferred to follow college games. Although the NFL had been around since the 1920s, the quality of play was inconsistent, the crowds were usually small, and teams occasionally would go out of business. This did not create much confidence in the sport's future.

What turned pro football around was television. As more and more Americans purchased TVs, more and more fans had a chance to watch NFL games. They got to know the different teams and players, many of whom were already familiar from their college days. By the 1960s, many fans started to prefer watching pro football. Network ratings became so strong that a new league was formed.

In 1960, the American Football League began its first season. The teams were owned by wealthy businessmen and were located in cities hungry for pro franchises. The AFL introduced several innovations that made the game easier and more exciting to watch. The league grabbed headlines by outbidding its NFL rivals for a handful of college stars. Most important, the AFL began play with a television contract. Its games were televised by ABC, which payed each team $150,000 as part of the agreement.

The AFL did not have much talent during its early years, but it made up for this deficiency with exciting, wide-open football. Starting in 1962, game attendance and

TV viewership began to climb dramatically. This made the NFL nervous. An all-out war over star players and key territories seemed unavoidable. Many NFL owners did not know how to fight this type of battle. Luckily, they had hired a commissioner who did.

Pete Rozelle, a smart young executive with the Los Angeles Rams in the 1950s, became the NFL's head man in 1960 after beloved commissioner Bert Bell died suddenly. Rozelle was not the first choice for the job; in fact, no one considered him a possibility at first. When the owners could not agree on a new commissioner, they reached a compromise and decided on Rozelle.

Rozelle understood the business of football as well as the power of television. He sensed before anyone else that the AFL would make it and that the upstart league would soon be challenging the NFL.

Pete Rozelle, the marketing "whiz kid" whose ability to see the big picture ushered in an era of great prosperity. He convinced NFL owners to merge with the AFL and made the Super Bowl the official championship of professional football.

Rather than plotting to crush the AFL, as many in the established league urged, Rozelle started making plans for the day when the two leagues would join forces. One of his first moves as commissioner was to convince the NFL owners to band together and sell their television rights as a "package." (Prior to that, each team negotiated with local stations.) By selling the entire league schedule to one network, each club made far more than it ever had in the past. NFL owners, convinced that Rozelle was a genius, gave him a long-term contract and happily followed his every suggestion.

By the mid-1960s, each league had a lucrative network television agreement in place. That meant every pro football team had lots of exposure and lots of money to spend. Rozelle knew that the only thing that could go wrong now would be a sharp rise in salaries. If the AFL and NFL continued to fight over the top college players, the players would be making millions while the owners teetered on the brink of financial ruin. In the spring of 1966, Rozelle saw his fears come true when a record $7 million was spent signing that year's top draft picks. It was time to bring the leagues together.

Rozelle made sure he treated the AFL as an equal. He knew that nothing good would come of trying to dominate the younger league, even though the NFL still had much more talent. Rozelle envisioned a new, larger pro football league that combined the tradition and stability of the NFL with the excitement and spirit of the AFL.

Rather than keeping AFL clubs down, Rozelle sought a plan that would quickly raise them to NFL levels. There were some bumps in the road, and some bruised egos, but by early June a merger agreement was hammered out. Part of that agreement called for an AFL-NFL "World Championship Game" to be played at the conclusion of the 1966 season. Soon everyone was calling this game the "Super Bowl."

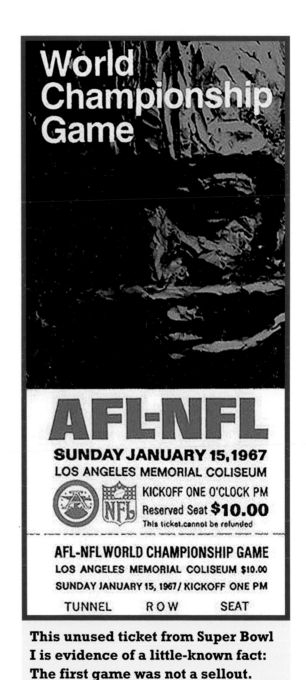

This unused ticket from Super Bowl I is evidence of a little-known fact: The first game was not a sellout.

COMPLETE SPORTS

60 STORIES ON THE 60 GREATEST STARS IN PRO FOOTBALL

50¢

sport heroes

MAC   **WINTER 1966**   BONUS: Statistics and Photo Of Each Player

JIM TAYLOR

PAUL HORNUNG

- JOHNNY UNITAS • GALE SAYERS • JOHN BRODIE • TIMMY BROWN
- JOE NAMATH • KEN WILLARD • BOB HAYES • TOMMY McDONALD
- RUDY BUKICH • PAUL LOWE • WAYNE WALKER • SONNY RANDLE
- RAY NITSCHKE • FRANK RYAN • LANCE ALWORTH • JACK KEMP
- SONNY JURGENSEN • TOMMY McDONALD • FRANK TARKENTON

The Kansas City Chiefs had to deal with Green Bay's "cover boys" in Super Bowl I. Jim Taylor (#31) was a human battering ram, while Paul Hornung (#5) was one of the best all-around players in history.

CHAPTER 1

THE 1960s

Super Bowl I
January 15, 1967
(1966 Season)
Green Bay Packers (NFL)
vs. Kansas City Chiefs (AFL)

The Green Bay Packers entered the 1966 season as defending league champions. A highly talented and deeply committed group of veterans, the Packers took the field supremely confident that their coach, taskmaster Vince Lombardi, would find a way to win. Endlessly drilled and driven to perfection, the team could make just about any game plan work. In 1965, Green Bay had beaten the Baltimore Colts in overtime to reach the NFL title game. The Packers then defeated Cleveland and its brilliant runner, Jim Brown, on a muddy field for the NFL championship. The 1966 Packers went 12-2 and earned a Super Bowl berth by beating the Dallas Cowboys in an exciting NFL title game, 34-27.

Despite its glittering regular-season record, Green Bay had seemed vulnerable going in against the Cowboys—a young, aggressive team that liked to play wide-open football. The Packers appeared to be growing old. Running backs Jim Taylor and Paul Hornung, whom Lombardi had used to spearhead the team's ground game, combined for a meager 905 yards. Elijah Pitts got plenty of carries, but he was most effective in short-yardage situations. A couple of high-priced rookies, Donny Anderson and Jim Grabowski, barely contributed at all.

At 33, quarterback Bart Starr was still at the peak of his powers, and he had an excellent year. But Green Bay was not a team that went to the air very often—on average about 20 times a game, and mostly in the form of quick tosses to Taylor, Pitts, and tight end Marv Fleming. Flanker Carroll Dale was Starr's primary long receiver. He had replaced veteran Max McGee after coming over in a deal with the Rams.

The Green Bay defense was tough and battle-tested. It was a mix of younger stars—linebacker Dave Robinson, pass-rusher Lionel Aldridge, and cornerback Herb Adderley—and old-timers such as end Willie Davis, tackle Henry Jordan, and safety Willie Wood. The leader of the pack was linebacker Ray Nitschke. A hard tackler who was also nimble enough to drop back into pass coverage, he sometimes seemed to be playing everywhere at once. Nitschke called the signals in the defensive huddle, and he almost always was in the right place when a fumble or deflected pass was up for grabs. He was a "money" player.

The Chiefs came into the big game with a marvelous collection of talent, although no one could quite gauge how they shaped up next to their NFL opponents. Quarterback Len Dawson, running back Mike Garrett, and receiver Otis Taylor clearly could have put up big numbers in the NFL. What was not clear was how the offense as a whole would fare against the mighty Packers.

The Kansas City defense begged similar questions. Linebacker Bobby Bell and defensive backs Johnny Robinson, Emmitt Thomas, and Fred "The Hammer" Williamson seemed capable of holding their own, but there was a significant drop-off in quality after that. The one sure thing the Chiefs had was defensive tackle Buck Buchanan, a monster who could single-handedly dominate the line of scrimmage. A former college sprinter, he stood at 6-foot-7 (2 meters) and weighed 290 pounds (132 kilograms). When Buchanan turned down an offer by the New York Giants to sign with the AFL out of Grambling State University in 1963, it was a major feather in the cap of the new league. It seemed only right that he play in the first Super Bowl.

The Chiefs fashioned an 11-2-1 record during the regular season, and they were a touchdown-per-game better than any other AFL team. They displayed their defensive grit in the AFL championship game, when they trounced the Buffalo Bills 31-7. Despite such a fine showing, no one outside of Kansas City thought the Chiefs would beat the Packers. The big debate was: Would the game even be close?

The Packers opened the scoring in the first quarter, when little-used McGee made a miraculous one-handed catch of a ball

thrown behind him. So stunned were the Kansas City backs that they could do little more than watch the veteran prance untouched into the end zone. The Chiefs struck back in the second quarter, when Dawson engineered a drive to the Green Bay 7-yard line and then threw for a score to running back Curtis McClinton.

The game did not remain tied for long. Starr came right back with a long drive of his own, and this culminated in a 14-yard touchdown run by Jim Taylor, who barreled right over several Kansas City tacklers. The Chiefs refused to surrender, however, and Mike Mercer made the score 14-10 on a 31-yard field goal right before the half.

The 61,946 fans in Los Angeles's Memorial Coliseum could hardly believe their eyes. Although in command, the Packers seemed to be struggling. They had beaten the NFL's best in ice, rain, and snow. Yet here, against the young, spirited Chiefs—in the warm air of Southern California—they could not pull away. In the locker room, Coach Lombardi was expressing similar thoughts to his players. He told them that the Chiefs would step on the field brimming with confidence in the second half, and that the Packers would simply have to beat it out of them.

With their pride on the line, the Packers came roaring out of the runway and onto the field for the second half. On defense, they overwhelmed the Kansas City offensive line by stuffing the run and terrorizing Dawson whenever he dropped back to pass. On offense, they made sharper cuts and crisper blocks. Slowly but surely, the Chiefs' confidence began to melt away.

The key play in the third quarter came when a frustrated Dawson chose to force a pass rather than to take a sack. The ball

TO THE MAX

In Super Bowl I, Green Bay fans could not have asked for a more unlikely hero than Max McGee. A favorite target of Bart Starr during the early 1960s, McGee had been a benchwarmer for two seasons, with just 14 passes in 1965 and 1966 combined. Although he had lost a step, McGee was still a sure-handed receiver who ran his routes with great precision. Off the field, he was the team comedian. He was also the unofficial champion of breaking curfew.

Normally, a player like McGee would not have been tolerated by Vince Lombardi, for whom discipline was everything. But the coach saw in McGee a team player who was always ready to deliver when called upon, and who could keep the Packers loose with a well-timed wisecrack or practical joke. Besides, he was the only guy who could make Lombardi laugh.

Figuring he would not play against the Chiefs, McGee went out and celebrated until the early hours on the eve of Super Bowl I. When he staggered into his hotel room and flopped on his bed, he had no idea what was awaiting him. Early in the game the next day, Green Bay's number-two wide receiver, Boyd Dowler, went out with an ankle injury. McGee was summoned from the bench and sent into the game in the fourth quarter with the Packers ahead 28-10. The Dallas secondary paid him little mind—and paid a high price. With the Packers needing an insurance score, Starr spotted McGee in the clear and drilled a perfect pass to him for a 28-yard touchdown, cementing a 35-10 victory. In all, McGee grabbed 7 passes for 138 yards and 2 touchdowns.

Max McGee pulls in one of his two touchdown receptions. The veteran, who had not expected to play, ended up playing a hero's role.

ended up in the capable hands of Wood, who ran it back to the 5-yard line. From there, Pitts swept into the end zone behind a wall of blockers to make the score 21-10. With Green Bay content to eat up the clock, Kansas City coach Hank Stram told his players to stop the run at all costs. Starr then crossed the Chiefs up by throwing a pass to McGee, who scored again on a 13-yard reception. Pitts added a second touchdown in the fourth quarter to make the final score 35-10.

The halftime adjustments made by the Packer staff had worked beautifully. The team exploited subtle weaknesses in the Kansas City line and secondary and maintained control of the ball throughout the second half. When the Chiefs got the ball, they were unable to move it. Kansas City did not mount a single scoring threat in the game's final 30 minutes. To their credit, however, they never gave up, hitting hard and going all out until the final gun sounded.

> **Packers 35**
> **Chiefs 10**
> Best Player: Bart Starr

Super Bowl II
January 14, 1968
(1967 Season)
Green Bay Packers (NFL)
vs. Oakland Raiders (AFL)

On the surface, the matchup for Super Bowl II was similar to that of the first championship game. The Green Bay Packers were NFL champions once again, while the Oakland Raiders—an exciting, confident team

from the AFL West—would continue the league's uphill battle for respect. The Packers, however, were not the same team as in years past. Gone were superstar runners Paul Hornung and Jim Taylor. They were replaced at first by Elijah Pitts and Jim Grabowski, both of whom fell to late-season injuries. Vince Lombardi, desperate to maintain his team's vaunted ground game, mixed and matched Donny Anderson, Chuck Mercein, Ben Wilson, and a meteoric kickoff-return specialist named Travis Williams, drafted out of Arizona State the previous spring.

Also gone from the Green Bay lineup was the zip that had been there in years past. Although a handful of players were entering their prime years, several veterans—particularly on defense—were slowing down. The Packers limped to a 9-4-1 record, just good enough to make the playoffs.

Then things changed. Green Bay knew how to win, and that came in handy in the postseason. It would take two victories to reach the Super Bowl, thanks to the reconfiguration of the NFL into four 4-team divisions. The Packers scored a comeback win over the L. A. Rams to advance to the title game, where once again they faced the Cowboys, who had demolished the Browns 52-14. With the game-time temperature at -13° Fahrenheit (-25° Celsius), the two teams fought the cold as hard as they fought each other. The Cowboys capitalized on three uncharacteristic Green Bay mistakes to build a 17-14 lead. With 4 minutes and 50 seconds left in the game, Starr took the Packers all the way to the Dallas 1-yard line. After Anderson failed to score twice, the Packers had time for one more play. Lombardi, refusing to kick the tying field goal, went for broke and called a quarterback sneak. Starr shouldered his way into the end zone to win what would forever be known as the "Ice Bowl."

Oakland's path to the ultimate game was far less dramatic, but the Raiders were pro football's most colorful team. Assembled by owner Al Davis with clever trades, good draft picks, and an appetite for misfits and renegades, the AFL champs rolled to a 13-1 record and easily beat the Houston Oilers in the title game. The Raiders rose to prominence on the arm of quarterback Daryle Lamonica; the toe of kicker George Blanda; and an offensive line, led by veteran Jim Otto and rookie Gene Upshaw, that punched out holes for a trio of slashing runners. The Oakland receiving corps featured a couple of glue-fingered stars named Fred Biletnikoff and Bill Miller. The Raider defense, nicknamed the "Eleven Angry Men," relied on defensive linemen Ben Davidson and Tom Keating and cornerbacks Kent McCloughan and Willie Brown. Duane Benson, a rookie who played like a maniac, was the team's X-factor at linebacker and on special teams.

In years past, the key element in almost every game involving the Green Bay Packers was how an opponent did against Lombardi's "power sweep." This was a bruising ballet that sent a group of five or six blockers sweeping toward the sideline in front of the team's star runners. In Super Bowl II, the shoe was on the other foot. If the Packers could not stop the power sweep of the Raiders, they stood a good chance of losing. Going into the game, however, the Packers had something else on their minds. Rumors were spreading that Coach Lombardi would leave coaching after this game, and he did not deny it. (Lombardi did leave the field and joined the Green Bay front office in

1968.) If there was ever a game that a group of players wanted to win for their coach, this was it.

For most of the first half, each team attempted to establish its running game. The Packers had some success, fashioning a 6-0 lead on two Don Chandler field goals, while the Raiders seemed stuck in neutral. With the ball on his own 38-yard line, Starr sent his receivers racing into the Oakland secondary. He knew that his primary target, 6-foot-5 (1.96-m) Boyd Dowler, towered over the Raiders' defensive backs, and thus might be able to outleap them for the ball. On this play, however, Dowler was all alone, and Starr hit him in stride for a 62-yard touchdown.

Behind 13-0, Lamonica got the Raiders on the scoreboard with a 23-yard touchdown pass to Miller. The defense held firm on the next series, forcing the Packers to punt from deep in their own territory. There was time for one more drive, perhaps even a touchdown, which would have sent Oakland into the locker room up 14-13. Return man Rodger Bird, normally sure-handed, signaled for a fair catch at midfield, then muffed the ball. The Packers recovered the fumble, and Starr slapped together a few quick plays to bring Green Bay within field-goal range. Chandler booted the ball through the uprights for a 16-7 lead and a huge shift in momentum.

As he had a year earlier, Lombardi reminded his troops at halftime how close this game really was. Then he discussed a few things that he wanted to do differently in the second half. As they had in Super Bowl I, the Packers came out and demolished their opponent in the third quarter. Starr led a magnificent, clock-eating drive that culminated in a 2-yard scoring plunge by Anderson.

STARR QUALITY

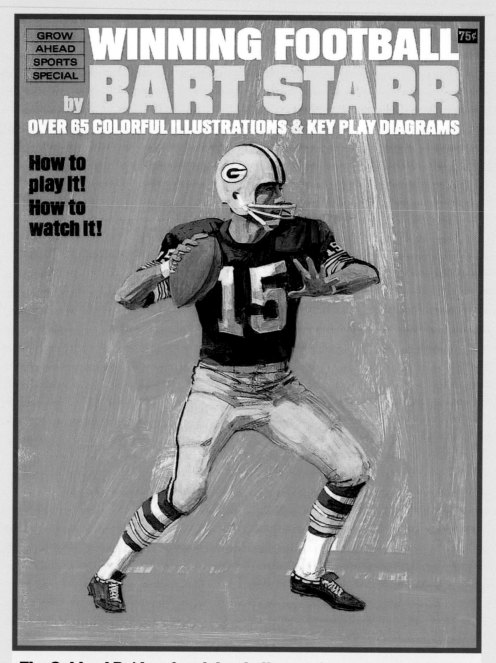

The Oakland Raiders faced the challenge of stopping Bart Starr, the man who literally wrote the book on winning football. During an eight-year stretch in the 1960s, he led the Packers to an 82-28 record in the regular season.

From 1960 to 1967, Vince Lombardi's Green Bay Packers had the best record in football, with 82 wins in 110 regular-season games. The man at the helm of the Green Bay offense was soft-spoken Bart Starr. No one knew it when coach and quarterback first met, but Starr was the ideal player for the job. Solid and consistent, he executed Lombardi's game plan to near perfection. Tough and talented, Starr could also rescue the team on those rare occasions when the Packers found themselves with their backs against the wall.

A 60 percent passer back in the days when most starters struggled to connect on half their attempts, Starr specialized in throwing medium-length balls for first downs. With Green Bay's productive ground game, there was little call for him to throw short passes. Because Lombardi liked to wear down opponents with long drives, Starr did not throw deep unless he had to. Even throwing only when he "had" to, Starr completed around a dozen passes a game, and he was rarely intercepted. In 1966, for instance, just 1.2 percent of his passes were picked off; in one stretch from 1964 to 1965, he attempted 294 passes without an interception. At his best in the big games, Starr was MVP of the first two Super Bowls.

Packer fans knew their quarterback was the right man at the right time. Outside Green Bay, however, Starr received only a fraction of the credit he deserved. Other quarterbacks, such as Johnny Unitas, John Brodie, and Roman Gabriel, were much flashier and far better at grabbing headlines. Also, it was widely known that Lombardi called most of the team's plays from the sideline. Thus Starr was cast as a robot who simply carried out his coach's instructions. (Today the coaches wouldn't have it any other way!) What few realized was that Starr had full authority to change plays in the huddle or at the line of scrimmage. When he did, the result was almost always a big success.

During Starr's 14 years as a starter, he led the league three times in completion percentage, and four times in fewest interceptions. Twice he recorded quarterback ratings above 100 and was named All-NFL four times between 1961 and 1966. The game and the quarterback position have changed dramatically in the years since Starr retired, yet he is still among the all-time leaders in a number of key categories. More impressive is the fact that no modern passer has equaled the three consecutive NFL championships he won from 1965 to 1967.

Over time, those who dismissed Starr came to appreciate him. The force of Lombardi's personality made even his best players seem insignificant at times, but in the end there was no hiding Starr's immense talents. Now historians believe that without number 15 under center, the Packers might never have reached the level of excellence they did.

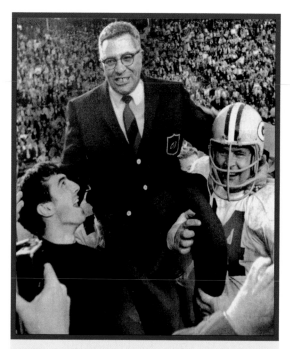

The architect of Green Bay's dynasty was head coach Vince Lombardi. Despite his strict, uncompromising style, he knew how to get the most from each of his players.

A second drive produced a fourth field goal by Chandler to make the score 26-7.

Any hope Oakland had of a comeback was erased in the fourth quarter, when Herb Adderley—the top cornerback in football—stepped in front of a Lamonica pass and returned it 60 yards for a score. The game's final touchdown was another 23-yard scoring pass from Lamonica to Miller, but by then it was way too late. Green Bay was the winner, 33-14.

Packers 33
Raiders 14
    Best Player: Bart Starr

Super Bowl III
January 12, 1969
(1968 Season)
Baltimore Colts (NFL)
vs. New York Jets (AFL)

What had begun as an exhibition game was now serious business. Rather than bringing the AFL and NFL closer, the Super Bowl had, in its first two years, served to illustrate just how far apart these two "business partners" were. The AFL's star players were every bit as good as the NFL's—this no one denied. But there seemed to be a huge drop-off when you got to the everyday starters and bench players. And because football is a team game, these players were crucial when it came to building competitive teams.

As an important part of the merger of the leagues, a handful of clubs from the NFL—to be renamed the National Football Conference, or NFC—moved over to the AFL, which would become the American Football Conference, or AFC. The NFC and AFC would play under the single banner of the NFL, with the two conference champions going to the Super Bowl. This was scheduled to occur in 1970. Originally, it was believed that the AFL would be able to close the talent gap by then, but Green Bay's Super Bowl massacres of the Chiefs and Raiders led many to question this plan. If every game between an NFL and AFL club was decided after a few minutes, who would buy tickets or even watch it on TV? The NFL owners were starting to get cold feet; one more blowout in the Super Bowl, and the entire deal might go down the drain.

Super Bowl III held little promise of solving this problem. The 1968 Colts ranked among the most impressive teams ever, while the AFL champion New York

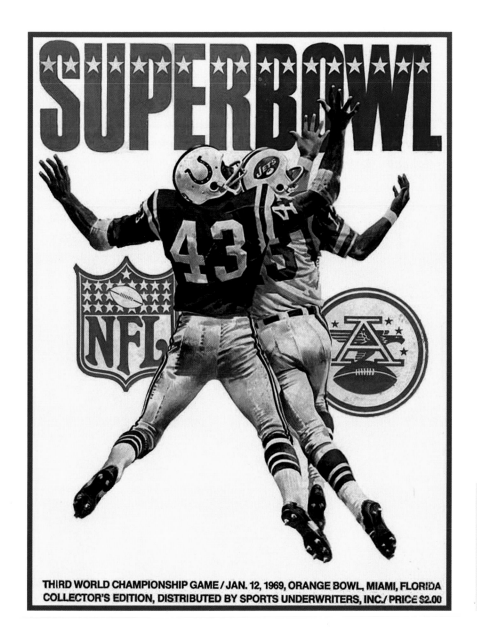

THIRD WORLD CHAMPIONSHIP GAME / JAN. 12, 1969, ORANGE BOWL, MIAMI, FLORIDA
COLLECTOR'S EDITION, DISTRIBUTED BY SPORTS UNDERWRITERS, INC./ PRICE $2.00

The program cover from Super Bowl III suggests that the Colts had the Jets covered. The real story turned out much differently.

Jets appeared to have less talent than the first two Super Bowl victims.

The Colts went 13-1 during the regular season, including a total of four wins over the powerful Rams and 49ers, who combined for just five other losses during the season. Baltimore also crushed Green Bay in the next-to-last game of the season, guaranteeing the Packers their first losing record since the 1950s.

The Colts were so good that not even a preseason injury to quarterback Johnny Unitas slowed them down. The team traded for veteran backup Earl Morrall, who stepped into a high-octane offense powered by running back Tom Matte, tight end John Mackey, and wide receivers Willie Richardson and Johnny Orr. Morrall tossed a league-high 26 touchdowns and was the NFL's top-ranked passer. The Baltimore

HEAD GAMES

Anyone who has ever played pro football will tell you that Super Bowl III was the greatest "psyche job" in the history of sports. Joe Namath's guarantee of a New York triumph was not a brash and boastful prediction. It was the carefully calculated first step in a remarkable, daring plan.

Joe Namath (#12) got the Colts so angry in the day prior to Super Bowl III, at times they seemed more intent on hurting him than tackling the ball carrier.

Namath was extremely talented and superconfident, but he knew the Jets would not stand a chance against the Colts without some kind of edge. His scheme was to so enrage the Colts with his insolence that they would stop doing the things they did well—containing opponents and controlling games—and try to separate the Jets' heads from their bodies.

The Colts had nothing to prove in Super Bowl III. They were the better team. Namath reasoned that if the Colts felt they did have something to prove, they might make themselves vulnerable to the younger, quicker Jets. To throw off the timing and judgment of the Baltimore veterans, Namath focused on the differences between the two clubs. The Colts were crew-cut, flag-waving, blue-collar types. They were a reflection of the hardworking city they represented. The Jets had long hair and sideburns, wore mod clothes, and fancied themselves suave and sophisticated. They were a reflection of the New York that offended older, more conservative people.

As the Jets' ringleader, Namath knew he was the perfect guy to get under the skin of the Colts' best players. He made a spectacle of himself in Miami in the week leading up to the game. He held court in the city's most popular nightclubs and conducted poolside press conferences in his bathing suit. When Namath guaranteed a New York victory, the Colts already despised him.

Namath knew his plan was working when he nearly came to blows with a group of Baltimore veterans in a Miami restaurant. The game was still a couple of days away, and the Colts were already losing their cool. Coach Weeb Ewbank did nothing to discourage his young quarterback. He not only sensed what Namath was up to, but also knew it would work. Ewbank had coached the Colts from 1954 to 1962 and was well acquainted with the team's leaders.

In order to beat Baltimore, Namath had to be willing not to play the game that had propelled the Jets to the Super Bowl in the first place. Throughout the season, Namath had specialized in the aerial attack. He threw for more than 3,000 yards and averaged nearly 17 yards per completion. He also made throws few others would dare to attempt. Namath rifled balls into heavy coverage, launched 50-yard bombs while on the run, and generally scared pass defenders out of their wits. For Super Bowl III, however, he decided to build his game plan around the threat of the pass rather than the pass itself. The poor Colts, playing back on their heels, never saw the aerial onslaught that they anticipated. The Jets' runners and possession receivers subtly dominated Baltimore from beginning to end.

defense was a *Who's Who* of hard-hitters: Bubba Smith, Mike Curtis, Bobby Boyd, Billy Ray Smith, Ordell Braase, Lou Michaels, and Jerry Logan, each among the elite at his position.

The Colts annihilated the Vikings and Browns in the playoffs, shutting out Cleveland 34-0 in the NFL championship game. The idea that Baltimore might soon be playing the majority of its games against AFL squads seemed unfair. The thought that the Colts might lose to the Jets was regarded as utterly absurd.

Except to Joe Namath. In the days leading up to the big game, the brash young Jets quarterback glibly predicted that he and his teammates would defeat the mighty Colts. In fact, he guaranteed it. Namath dismissed the vaunted Baltimore defense as overrated, then rattled off the names of five AFL quarterbacks (including his own) whom he ranked higher than Morrall.

Namath was more talented than Morrall. After that, however, the head-to-head matchups appeared to favor the Colts. New York's other stars were running backs Matt Snell and Emerson Boozer. They were good, but neither was a game breaker. The Jets' top receiver, Don Maynard, was better than anything the Colts had, but he would be double-teamed by a pair of Baltimore Pro Bowl defensive backs. The offensive line was younger and smaller than the Colt pass rushers, while the defense was little more than a collection of well-coached journeymen. They had won many games by capitalizing on enemy mistakes. Unfortunately, the Colts did not make many mistakes.

As luck would have it, they made their first mistake early in Super Bowl III. After driving deep into New York territory, the Colts muffed three chances to score a touchdown. Then Michaels, who doubled as the team's placekicker, missed his field-goal try. Instead of grabbing a quick lead and establishing dominance as they had so many times during the year, Baltimore came away empty.

The Jets, meanwhile, were gaining confidence. The Baltimore players were angry and edgy. They were too aggressive at times, actually running themselves out of plays they usually made. The smaller, younger Jets were also a little quicker off the ball; after each snap, the New Yorkers were in motion a fraction of a second before their opponents. And when bodies collided, the Jets gave as good as they got. On one play, Snell took the ball into the line and was met by safety Rick Volk. Snell kept right on going, and Volk staggered off the field, disoriented. The Colts suddenly did not seem so tough.

Meanwhile, their bad luck continued. After recovering a fumble on the Jets' 12-yard line, the Colts tried twice to run the ball across the goal line without success. Then Morrall fired a perfect pass to end Tom Mitchell. Linebacker Al Atkinson ticked the ball with his finger, redirecting it just enough to throw off Mitchell. The ball struck Mitchell's shoulder pad and bounced high in the air. New York cornerback Randy Beverley made a headlong dive in the end zone and intercepted the ball before it hit the turf.

Two mistakes had cost Baltimore ten points. Now Namath decided it was time to make the Colts pay. Reading the Colts' defensive schemes perfectly, he ran the ball when they were in pass coverage, passed the ball when they came up to counter the run, and dumped off short passes when

Baltimore blitzed. On every play, the Jets hit first and hit harder. They totally controlled the game. A few minutes later, Snell punctuated a drive that went the length of the field when he barreled into the end zone. The Colts, confused and humiliated, looked at one another trying to figure out what had just happened. A strange hush fell over Miami's Orange Bowl. Even the Jets fans were in awe of what they had just witnessed.

The Colts regrouped and threatened New York again. Matte broke off a 58-yard run to put Baltimore within striking distance of the Jets' goal line. Once again the defense held. Ex-Colt Johnny Sample, the unit's fast-talking, in-your-face veteran, picked off a Morrall pass and then taunted his former teammates as millions watched in disbelief.

The Colts held and got the ball back. Once again, Morrall maneuvered his team across midfield. As time ticked away on the first half, he called a "flea-flicker." This play starts with the quarterback giving the ball to a runner, hoping to draw the defensive backs toward the line. The runner then whirls and laterals it back to the quarterback, who hopes to find a wide-open receiver downfield. The play worked to perfection. Safety Jim Hudson had taken the bait and was 20 yards off his man, Jimmy Orr, who was waving frantically for the ball with no one remotely near him. Unfortunately for the Colts, the Baltimore band, in preparation for its halftime performance, had taken a position behind the end zone. When Morrall looked toward the goal line, he was unable to pick out Orr from the sea of blue-and-white uniforms. Instead, he fired the ball to Jerry Hill, who had also shaken his man. The moment the ball left

his fingers, Morrall knew he had made a terrible mistake. Hudson, way out of position to defend Orr, was in the perfect place to step in front of the pass to Hill, which he did. For the fourth time in the first half, Baltimore had squandered a great scoring chance.

The Colts, a three-touchdown favorite in this game, went into the locker room in a state of shock. Not only were they behind 7-0, but they had missed chances to score as many as 28 points! While New York coach Weeb Ewbank praised his players and coolly explained how they would build on their lead in the second half, Baltimore's Don Shula raged at his Colts. They had made a dozen dumb mistakes and had learned nothing about the Jets in 30 minutes. Far worse, the Jets no longer feared them. "You've got them believing in themselves," screamed Shula. "You've got them thinking they're better than we are!"

Any chance the Colts had of reestablishing control in the third quarter was lost when Matte fumbled his first carry of the half on the 33-yard line. Namath moved the Jets within field-goal range, and kicker Jim Turner split the uprights to make the score 10-0. Knowing the Colts needed two scores to catch them, the Jets were now relaxed and confident. The Colts, on the other hand, were beginning to panic. The defense was in such a state of confusion that it failed to realize that Namath had badly hurt the thumb on his throwing hand after a hard tackle. Backup Babe Parilli came in and ran the team for a series while Namath tested his thumb, and the Jets got another field goal to make the score 13-0. When Namath returned, he could barely throw. The Colts continued to drop back into coverage, however, fearful that Broadway Joe would burn them with one of his patented 50-yard bombs.

With Morrall's confidence sapped, Shula called on Unitas, his injured star, to come in and rescue the team. Unitas managed to get the Colts on the scoreboard with a touchdown, but by then the Jets had added another field goal and eaten up the clock.

The game ended 16-7, and pro football was saved. Had the Colts done to the Jets what the Green Bay Packers had done to the Chiefs and the Raiders, the merger might have been called off. Had that occurred, the two leagues would have been at each other's throats, sending salaries and ticket prices spiraling out of control. Instead, the football world looked upon the AFL with respect and even admiration. Now the worst anyone could say was that the AFL was David to the NFL's Goliath—an arrangement that fans and owners could accept until the talent gap disappeared for good.

Jets 16
Colts 7
Best Player: Joe Namath

CHAPTER 2

THE 1970s

Super Bowl IV
January 11, 1970
(1969 Season)
Minnesota Vikings (NFL)
vs. Kansas City Chiefs (AFL)

In Super Bowl IV, the Kansas City Chiefs had an opportunity to prove that the astonishing victory by the New York Jets had not been a fluke. Here, in the last Super Bowl that featured a meeting between AFL and NFL champions, the Chiefs took on the heavily favored Minnesota Vikings.

Kansas City had evolved into the AFL's toughest team since its first Super Bowl appearance in 1967. Under no-nonsense coach Hank Stram, its core of stars was older, wiser, and more focused on what it had to do to win close ball games. The offense was nothing to brag about, yet it was good enough both to score and to chew up the clock when necessary. Len Dawson, 35, was nearing the end of the line. He often gave way to 23-year-old Mike Livingston, who did a whale of a job in a backup role. Running back Mike Garrett saw the ball the most, gaining 732 yards on 168 carries and catching 43 passes. Robert Holmes and Warren McVea also proved capable ball carriers.

The Chiefs lived and died by their de-fense, which could be suffocating. Buck Buchanan, Bobby Bell, Jerry Mays, Johnny Robinson, and Emmitt Thomas—all holdovers from the 1966 team—were joined by young tackle Curly Culp and the relentless Willie Lanier, a linebacker who moved around the field like a lion roams the savannah. The Chiefs finished second in the AFL West but won the league crown by defeating the Jets and Raiders in the playoffs by a combined score of 30-13.

The Vikings were very similar to the Chiefs. They, too, relied on their defense to win games. Minnesota's linemen—Alan Page, Carl Eller, Jim Marshall, and Gary Larsen—were equally good against the run and the pass. The linebacking crew, led by Wally Hilgenberg, was young and aggressive. And the defensive backs were deadly, with Paul Krause and Bobby Bryant leading a group that intercepted 22 passes.

Minnesota's offense was led by quarterback Joe Kapp, a player who got the job done on three parts determination and one part talent. The tandem of Dave Osborn and Bill Brown handled the running game, while Gene Washington was Kapp's favorite downfield receiver. The Vikings' offense was hardly high-powered, but the defense kept giving it the ball. That put the pressure on kicker Fred Cox, who responded with an amazing 121 points on 26 field goals and 43 extra points.

The experts predicted that this game would be a battle for control of the line of scrimmage. They believed the Kansas City defense could contain Kapp but felt the Viking front four would simply overwhelm the Chiefs. During a hard-fought first quarter, Kansas City's offensive line held its own and Jan Stenerud kicked a long field goal to give the Chiefs a 3-0 lead. In the second quarter, the tactic of double-teaming the defensive ends, Eller and Marshall, turned the tide for the Chiefs. Dawson was able to move the ball, and he set up a second Stenerud field goal. The Chiefs made it 9-0 on a third field goal after Minnesota's David Lee shanked a punt to give Kansas City good field position.

Disaster struck for the Vikings on the ensuing kickoff, when young Charlie West fumbled the ball and Dawson directed a quick scoring drive to make the score 16-0. At the half, Kansas City was in total control.

Minnesota coach Bud Grant hoped the Chiefs would become complacent with their big lead and let up in the second half. In the Kansas locker room, however, the Chiefs were more determined to thrash the Vikings than when the game started. One of Minnesota's goals in the game was to try to put Dawson out. Eller and Page took every opportunity to hit him, even after he had thrown the ball. This angered the Chiefs, who vowed to protect their beloved quarterback.

After holding the Chiefs on their first possession of the second half, the Vikings made their best drive of the game. Starting

Otis Taylor is embraced by teammate Mike Garrett after making the game-breaking play in Super Bowl IV. The Chiefs scored a second straight upset for the AFL.

LENNY KEEPS 'EM GUESSING

When Len Dawson watched game films of the Minnesota Vikings while preparing for Super Bowl IV, he might have been the only man in the room who liked what he saw. Bud Grant's hard-hitting, fierce-tackling defense moved like a swarm of purple bees around the football, anticipating an opponent's every move and enveloping the ball carrier just as he seemed to find some running room. The Vikings gave up a mere 158 points in 1969, which was a tribute to the skill of the players and the preparation of Coach Grant. Dawson spotted a weakness, however. The Vikings never expected the unexpected. Whenever a quarterback called an unusual play, the Minnesota defense seemed to lose its rhythm for a play or two.

During Super Bowl IV, Dawson used this discovery to great advantage. When he sensed the Vikings were getting into a groove, he would call a weird play just to throw them off. Sometimes he would run a basic play that did not fit a particular situation. On three occasions, Dawson called a "flanker-around" for Frank Pitts, a receiver who had taken just five handoffs during the year. Although none of these plays gained much yardage, each kept the Minnesota defense from finding its comfort zone. Dawson later said this was one of the keys to moving the ball against the "Purple People Eaters."

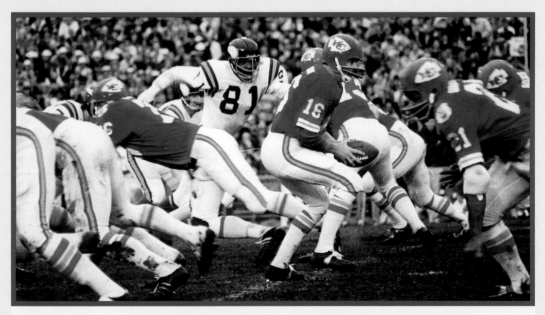

Kansas City quarterback Len Dawson kept Minnesota off-balance throughout Super Bowl IV with his unconventional play calling. The Vikings were beaten to the punch time and time again.

on their own 31-yard line, they worked their way down the field and scored on a short run by Dave Osborn. The score was now 16-7. Kapp was having a hard time handling the Kansas City pass rush, but he still managed to complete most of his throws. The Vikings were not out of it yet.

Any chance the Vikings had of narrowing the gap vanished a few minutes later. Dawson dropped back to pass around midfield, spotted a Minnesota blitz, and dumped the ball out to receiver Otis Taylor, whose man slipped. Taylor spun upfield, sidestepped a couple of tacklers, and darted down the sideline for a magnificent touchdown.

The Vikings were done for good when Kapp had to leave the game with a separated shoulder. After a scoreless final quarter, the Chiefs were 23-7 winners—and world champions.

> **Chiefs 23**
> **Vikings 7**
> Best Player: Len Dawson

Super Bowl V
January 17, 1971
(1970 Season)
Dallas Cowboys (NFC)
vs. Baltimore Colts (AFC)

The Baltimore Colts, Pittsburgh Steelers, and Cleveland Browns moved to the American Football Conference for the 1970 season as part of the merger agreement between the AFL and the NFL. When Baltimore emerged as AFC champion, no one was surprised. The Colts were unquestionably the class of the conference. Their meet-

ing with NFC champion Dallas Cowboys promised to be the best Super Bowl yet.

The move to the AFC was not a bad one for the Colts. In 1969, they had been in a division that included the powerhouse Rams and rapidly improving 49ers. Now the Colts got to play six games against the Patriots, Bills, and Jets, who together managed a total of nine wins all season. They also played two games against the Miami Dolphins, a 3-win team in 1969 that improved to 10-4 after hiring Don Shula. The Colts, under soft-spoken coach Don McCaffrey, finished 11-2-1 and beat the Bengals and the Raiders in the playoffs to earn a Super Bowl berth.

Johnny Unitas, back in command for the Colts, hooked up with receivers Roy Jefferson, Eddie Hinton, and John Mackey for 119 catches and 15 touchdowns during the 1970 season. Norm Bulaich and Tom Nowatzke filled in for an injured Tom Matte and did a fine job. As always, the Baltimore defense was exceptional, with future Hall of Famers Bubba Smith, Ted Hendricks, and Mike Curtis leading the way.

The Cowboys countered with one of the most talented rosters in football, although the team did not always live up to its potential. Head coach Tom Landry had three capable running backs in Calvin Hill, Walt Garrison, and Duane Thomas. His passing attack, which featured Bob Hayes—a former Olympic sprinter who tended to drop easy passes—was the team's weak point. Quarterback Craig Morton, battling a shoulder injury, threw less and less as the season wore on anyway.

On the other side of the ball, the acquisition of former Green Bay superstar Herb Adderley beefed up a defensive secondary that would soon be recognized as one of the greatest ever. Adderley, Mel Renfro, and rookies Charlie Waters and Cliff Harris limited the Cowboys' opponents to fewer than 15 completions a game. Rushing enemy passers were veterans Bob Lilly and Jethro Pugh, who were backed up by linebackers Lee Roy Jordan and Chuck Howley. The "Doomsday Defense" promised to give Unitas fits.

Midway through the first quarter, the Cowboys produced the game's first turnover. With Baltimore threatening, Howley dropped into coverage and intercepted a pass by Unitas, returning it to midfield. Then Morton lost 23 yards on the next three plays, and Ron Widby came on to punt. The game's second turnover came moments later, when return man Ron Gardin fumbled and Harris dove on the ball inside the Colts' 10-yard line. The Baltimore defense held, however, and the Cowboys had to settle for a field goal by Mike Clark and a 3-0 lead.

Clark kicked another three-pointer in the second quarter, but the Colts got back in the game on one of the most controversial plays in Super Bowl history. Throwing from deep in his own territory, Unitas hummed a pass to Hinton. The ball was too high, and Hinton could do little more than deflect it away. Renfro, in position to intercept the pass, strained to reach it when it changed direction. Game films later showed he grazed the ball with his fingernail. Running all the way on this play was Mackey, the big tight end. No one was more surprised than he when the ball found its way into his hands. At the time, NFL rules prohibited two offensive players from touching the ball without a defensive player touching in between, so Renfro's role was crucial. Mackey did not hang around to wait for the official's decision. He ran the length of the field to complete the 75-yard scoring play, which

knotted the score at 6-6. Dallas blocked Jim O'Brien's extra-point attempt to preserve the tie.

The comedy of errors continued when Unitas coughed up the ball at his own 28-yard line on Baltimore's next possession. Morton pounced on this opportunity. After moving the Cowboys to the 7-yard line, he threw a short pass to Thomas, who crossed the goal line to give Dallas the lead. Unitas's troubles continued. Defensive end George Andrie crashed into him in midpass, causing him to throw his third interception. Even worse, his ribs were badly bruised, and Unitas had to leave the game.

Backup Earl Morrall entered the game on Baltimore's next series, and he moved the team quickly. The veteran fired long passes to Jefferson and Hinton, giving the Colts a first-and-goal on the Dallas 2-yard line. Three times he sent Bulaich into the line, and three times the Cowboys kept him out of the end zone. On fourth down, Morrall tried a short pass to Tom Mitchell, but it fell incomplete. The Cowboys took a shaky 13-6 lead into the locker room.

Baltimore wasted no time in committing the first mistake of the second half. Jim Duncan fumbled the opening kickoff, and Dallas had a chance to build a nice cushion. Then, six plays later, the Cowboys gave the break back. Thomas, met by tacklers at the goal line, made a desperate second effort to score. Somewhere in the tangle of bodies, a Baltimore player jarred the ball loose, and Duncan, playing cornerback, made up for his earlier mistake by recovering the loose ball.

Neither team was able to make much progress until midway through the fourth quarter. With the score still 13-6 in favor of the Cowboys, Morrall decided to call a flea-flicker—the same play that many felt wrecked the Colts in Super Bowl III against the Jets. Morrall pitched out to running back Sam Havrilak, who took a few steps and then spun to lateral the ball back to Morrall. He thought better of this when he saw that the immense Pugh had sniffed out the play and was closing fast. Havrilak, a quarterback in college, decided to improvise. He saw Mackey open and threw the ball in his direction. Before the pass reached the tight end, Hinton plucked it out of the air and raced through the Dallas secondary, which was now in total disarray. Safety Cornell Green, in hot pursuit of Hinton, came up behind the receiver and punched the ball out of his hands. More madness followed, as the football skittered toward the end zone with six players trying to run it down. It crossed the goal line and tumbled out of the end zone. The referee ruled the play a touchback, giving the ball to the Cowboys on their own 20-yard line.

Dallas fans had barely stopped cheering when disaster struck. Morton faded back and threw to Walt Garrison, who was coming out of the backfield. Duncan read the play and was able to tip the ball. Rick Volk caught the ball and returned it 30 yards to the Dallas 3-yard line. From there, Nowatzke punched it in to even the game at 13-13.

With time winding down, it looked as if the Super Bowl was headed into overtime. Dallas had the ball in its own territory, and its offense had done nothing in the second half. Morton attempted to hit running back Dan Reeves with a short pass. Curtis, Baltimore's middle linebacker, picked it off and returned it to the 28-yard line. In those days, when the goalposts were located at the front of the end zone, this put a field goal well

within the range of O'Brien, a nervous rookie who, years earlier, had to leave the Air Force Academy because of ulcers. Morrall sent Bulaich into the line twice to get the ball a few yards closer, then called time-out.

O'Brien trotted on the field to face the biggest moment of his life. With his teammates imploring him to relax and the Cowboys taunting him to break his concentration, O'Brien—a straight-on kicker—lined it up and let it fly. The ball sailed through the

Baltimore kicker Jim O'Brien jumps for joy. His field goal with time running out won the contest for the Colts.

GREAT GAME, SORRY YOU LOST

Chuck Howley's wife looks happier than he does about the Dodge Charger awarded to the Super Bowl MVP. Howley would have preferred a victory over the Colts.

The Super Bowl MVP Award is one of the most coveted in all of sports. It means that, on the day it mattered most, you were the best player on the best team in all of football. At least, that is what it is supposed to mean. How do you give an award to someone on a team that made more dumb mistakes than any winning team ever made in a championship game?

The Colts' candidates for the Super Bowl V MVP Award did not exactly stand out. The quarterbacks, Johnny Unitas and Earl Morrall, were unable to make big plays when they had to. Baltimore's running backs got crushed every time they touched the ball. John Mackey's long touchdown was more luck than skill, and he caught just one other pass all day. Jim O'Brien, the kicker, was the happiest man on the field when he won the game. He would not have had to make that kick, however, had he not drilled his extra-point attempt into the chest of Dallas's Mark Washington back in the second quarter. On the defensive side, no one Colt stood out except for Jim Duncan, but his fumbled kickoff to start the second half had nearly cost Baltimore the game. Not even his jarring tackle on Duane Thomas moments later produced a worthy MVP—replays showed that three Colts had hit Thomas at once.

So, when it came time to present the MVP trophy, the ceremony took place in the losing locker room!

Much to his surprise, linebacker Chuck Howley of the Cowboys was voted the game's top player. His two interceptions represented the only positive statistic of the entire game! "The award is tremendous," Howley told the smattering of reporters given the task of covering the Cowboy locker room. "But I wish it were the world championship."

uprights with 5 seconds remaining, giving the Colts a 16-13 victory.

More than three decades later, Super Bowl V still stands as one of the most exciting—and also one of the worst-played—championship contests in sports history. Despite the presence of two well-coached veteran squads, the game featured six fumbles, six interceptions, and a botched extra point.

> **Colts 16**
> **Cowboys 13**
>   Best Player: Chuck Howley

Super Bowl VI
January 16, 1972
(1971 Season)
Dallas Cowboys (NFC)
vs. Miami Dolphins (AFC)

Super Bowl VI was a battle between two of football's greatest coaches and a couple of very different teams. For several years, Tom Landry's Dallas Cowboys had as much talent as anyone in the NFL, but each season his club fell short of the championship. Twice, Dallas's dream of a title had been snatched from them on the final play of the game. Meanwhile, Don Shula's Miami Dolphins were the success story of the AFC. Lured away from his job with the Colts in 1970 by Miami owner Joe Robbie, Shula had turned a 3-10-1 loser into a 10-3-1 conference champion in just two seasons.

The Cowboys of Super Bowl VI were basically the same team that battled the Colts in Super Bowl V. The one important change of the 1971 season came at quarter-

Dallas returned to the Super Bowl again in 1972. This time Tom Landry looked to quarterback Roger Staubach to lead the offense.

back. For the first half of the season, Landry alternated Craig Morton and Roger Staubach. Morton had more experience, but Staubach had more talent, and eventually Staubach won out. Installed as the regular in week 8, "Roger the Dodger" threw and scrambled his way to seven straight wins to close out the year.

The Dallas receiving corps got a further boost from the addition of two solid veterans, Lance Alworth and Mike Ditka. At the same time that Staubach grabbed the starting job, Duane Thomas returned to form after holding out in a salary dispute. Backed by the steady play of the "Doomsday Defense," the Cowboys came into the Super Bowl looking unbeatable.

The Dolphins did have a chance.

NICE CALL, MR. PRESIDENT

President Richard Nixon was a big football fan and a die-hard supporter of the Washington Redskins. As a sometime-resident of Florida, Nixon's second-favorite team was the Miami Dolphins. After the Dolphins shut out the Colts in the AFC title game, Nixon phoned Don Shula to talk strategy.

In his estimation, Nixon offered, the Dallas defense would be vulnerable to a deep pass over the middle to Paul Warfield. Shula agreed—what else could he do? He even added the play to the Miami offense just for the Super Bowl. Imagine the president's surprise when, late in the first quarter, Griese called the "Nixon Play." Imagine his disappointment when the pass fell incomplete. The Cowboys read the route instantly. Mel Renfro and Cliff Harris had Warfield double-covered all the way.

President Richard Nixon, sitting beside Attorney General John Mitchell, waves to a friend during Super Bowl VI. A rabid football fan, Nixon actually designed a play that the Dolphins used during the game.

Shula's team boasted one of the most versatile offenses in football. Fullback Larry Csonka, a human battering ram, was the first 1,000-yard runner to appear in a Super Bowl. His backfield mates, Jim Kiick and Mercury Morris, were quick and clever. Quarterback Bob Griese, the AFC's top-rated passer in 1971, threw short to Kiick and long to veteran Paul Warfield, one of the best deep-threat receivers in NFL history. A trio of young offensive linemen—Jim Langer, Larry Little, and Bob Kuechenberg—matured quickly under Shula and provided ample protection for Miami's offensive stars.

The Dolphin defense was deeply talented but inexperienced. Linebacker Nick Buoniconti was the only man on the entire unit older than 29. But Miami held tough when it had to. In the playoffs, the defense contained the Chiefs in a thrilling double-overtime game, then shut out the mighty Colts 21-0 to win the AFC championship. Stopping Dallas would not be so easy, however.

Experience set the tone for the day, beginning with Miami's second series. Csonka, who had not fumbled all year, bobbled a handoff from Griese, and when the referee's whistle blew, Chuck Howley of the Cowboys was cradling the football. It was a crucial mistake. Not only did Dallas take over with great field position, but Csonka had fumbled on a play when his blockers had opened a magnificent hole for him. Staubach moved the ball into field-goal range, and Mike Clark booted it through the uprights for a 3-0 lead.

In the second quarter, Griese decided to take to the air. He soon discovered what the Cowboys' other opponents knew all too well: You just don't go there. On one play, the Miami quarterback found all of his receivers covered and Bob Lilly bearing down on him. With the crowd cheering wildly, Griese zigzagged all over the field. Unfortunately, he was going the wrong way. Underestimating the speed and agility of the 260-pound (118-kg) Lilly, Griese was tackled for a 29-yard loss. On offense, Dallas also wore out the Dolphins. Midway through the period, Staubach marched his troops 76 yards for a touchdown, finishing with a 7-yard strike to Alworth.

Down 10-0 with less than 2 minutes to go in the second quarter, Griese gave Miami fans hope with a quick drive to the Dallas 23-yard line. From there, Garo Yepremian booted a field goal to cut the deficit to seven points. Shula went into the locker room believing his team could win. Keep Staubach in check, he told Buoniconti, and Griese would eventually solve the Dallas defense.

The second half did not go as planned for the Dolphins. Dallas took the opening kickoff and went 71 yards in 8 plays to make the score 17-3. Long runs by Duane Thomas and Bob Hayes caught the Miami defense by surprise and seemed to rob the Dolphins of their desire. In the fourth quarter, Howley finished off Miami when he ducked in front of Kiick at midfield and intercepted a flair pass from Griese. Running unchallenged toward the end zone, the MVP of the previous year's contest fell flat on his face as he crossed the 10-yard line. Three plays later, however, Staubach threw a touchdown pass to Ditka and sealed Miami's doom. The game ended 24-3.

Cowboys 24
Dolphins 3
   Best Player: Roger Staubach

Super Bowl VII
January 14, 1973
(1972 Season)
Washington Redskins (NFC)
vs. Miami Dolphins (AFC)

For the first time since Joe Namath and the Jets took on the powerhouse Baltimore Colts, the Super Bowl offered a story that fans could really sink their teeth into. The Miami Dolphins returned for a second run at the championship, this time without a single defeat. The creaky, quirky Washington Redskins were their improbable opponents. Would the Dolphins pull off the modern era's first perfect season? Or would the Redskins' "Over the Hill Gang" steal a victory, as they had all season long?

Everything clicked for the Dolphins in 1972. Larry Csonka and Mercury Morris became the first backfield mates to top 1,000 yards apiece. The offensive line, made up entirely of players cut from other teams, had perhaps the greatest season of any front five. The team's "No-Name Defense" held opponents to the fewest points in the NFL, and 38-year-old Earl Morrall, called upon to fill the injured Bob Griese's shoes, turned in an MVP season. Don Shula's team won all 14 of its regular-season games, and only three of those contests were even close. After defeating the Browns and Steelers in the playoffs, they were ready for anyone.

The Washington Redskins had one thing going for them against this awesome opponent: They were completely unlike any team the Dolphins had faced. Coached by master motivator George Allen, Washington overcame an early-season injury to quarterback Sonny Jurgensen, one of the best throwers in football. His replacement, Billy

Kilmer, was one of the worst. He had been called upon to fill in for Jurgensen in 1971 as well, and he got the job done. In 1972, Kilmer had a terrific year, leading the conference with 19 touchdown passes.

The Washington offense was keyed by halfback Larry Brown, the most relentless rusher in the league. Kilmer's job was to hand the ball to Brown until opponents became obsessed with stopping him. Then Kilmer would launch wobbly passes to speedy veterans Roy Jefferson and Charley Taylor and tight end Jerry Smith, who had a career year.

The Redskins' defense featured a collection of banged-up veterans, many acquired for little or nothing from other teams: Verlon Biggs, Ron McDole, Diron Talbert, Chris Hanburger, Jack Pardee, Myron Pottios, Pat Fischer, Brig Owens, Richie Petitbon, and Rosey Taylor. Somehow, this group pulled together and held enemy offenses to just 218 points. The Dolphins had lost to an "experienced" club a year before, but this was ridiculous!

The pressure was all on the Dolphins. Shula knew that if Miami lost this game, the team would not be remembered for its 16-1 season. They would be branded as losers. This made the decision of which quarterback to start an agonizing one. Earl Morrall was Player of the Year, but Griese was healthy again and seemingly in fine form. Returning to the field for the first time in nearly three months, he had tossed a pair of clutch touchdown passes against the Steelers in the AFC championship game. With a few days to go, Shula named Griese his starter.

Shula believed his defense matched up perfectly against the Redskins. Confident that his four defensive backs could cover

Washington's receivers, he ordered his front seven to concentrate on plugging up Brown's running lanes and rushing Kilmer when he dropped back to pass. The rest would take care of itself.

The Redskins came out strong, but Miami broke through first. On their third possession of the game, the Dolphins crossed midfield and reached the Washington 30. On third down, Griese called for a pass play. While the Redskins concentrated on Warfield, Howard Twilley—who had been with the team since its first season in 1966—beat Fischer and hauled in a perfect pass at the 5-yard line for a touchdown.

The two teams continued to slug it out in the second quarter, with both playing well on defense. Then, with time running out, Kilmer was intercepted by Buoniconti, who returned the ball to Washington's 27-yard line. Five plays later, Jim Kiick scored on a 1-yard run to give Miami a 14-0 lead.

With the exception of some untimely penalties, the Dolphins' game plan had thus far worked to perfection. They returned to the field in the second half cool and confident. The Redskins knew they were in trouble. Miami's left defensive tackle, Manny Fernandez, was playing the game of his life; he had completely shut down the line of scrimmage. No matter where he ran, Brown was met by a gang of Dolphin tacklers. Washington could do little more than play tough defense and hope for a lucky bounce.

The Redskins managed to mount two significant drives in the second half, but neither resulted in any points. The first occurred early in the third quarter, but Kilmer threw two incompletions and then was sacked by Fernandez. Kicker Curt Knight, who went 7-for-7 in Washington's two playoff victories, missed a 32-yarder. In the fourth quarter, Kilmer maneuvered the Redskins down to the 10-yard line. Then safety Jake Scott intercepted a pass in the end zone and returned it to midfield, seemingly ending any chance for Washington to get back in the game.

Finally, Washington got its lucky bounce. After advancing to the 35-yard line, the Dolphins sent the field-goal unit on the field for a 42-yard try. Yepremian's kick was low, and the Redskins easily blocked it. The ball bounced back to the small soccer-style kicker, who looked up to see a snorting, snarling wave of burgundy and gold charging toward him. In a panic, he tried to throw the ball—something he apparently had never

Miami safety Jake Scott tips a pass during Super Bowl VII. His clutch plays on defense prevented the Redskin offense from scoring.

SIDEKICKS

Throughout the history of pro football, placekickers have suffered from an image problem. The game is named after what they do, yet they are only on the field for a minute or two, and rarely do they get their uniforms dirty. Often, their own teammates do not consider them real players. That is why, for many years, pro coaches shied away from using specialists. Instead, stars who played other positions handled kicking duties.

In 1964, a Hungarian refugee named Pete Gogolak was signed to kick for the Buffalo Bills. Despite being a newcomer to football, he scored 102 points and was a major contributor to Buffalo's AFL championship. Gogolak's kicking prowess came from a lifetime of soccer, and he booted the ball like no American kicker ever had—sideways. Fans fell in love with Gogolak and his weird soccer-style kicking. He was so popular that the NFL reportedly plotted to steal him away from the AFL—a move that pushed both leagues closer to their historic merger agreement.

By the early 1970s, several more soccer-style kickers had established themselves in the pros. These included Jan Stenerud, Horst Muhlman, Roy Gerela, Bobby Howfield, and Pete's brother, Charlie. Besides their strange style, they had one other thing in common: unlike the old-timers, they couldn't do anything but kick. This became a running joke among NFL fans.

Nothing was funnier than Garo Yepremian's predicament in Super Bowl VII. The last thing the Miami kicker expected when his field-goal attempt was blocked was to find the football in his possession. As the Redskins closed in on Yepremian, his life must have flashed before his eyes—and in no part of that life had he actually thrown a football. This became obvious when he attempted his disastrous pass. The ball fluttered a few feet before Mike Bass plucked it out of the air and raced past Yepremian for Washington's only touchdown.

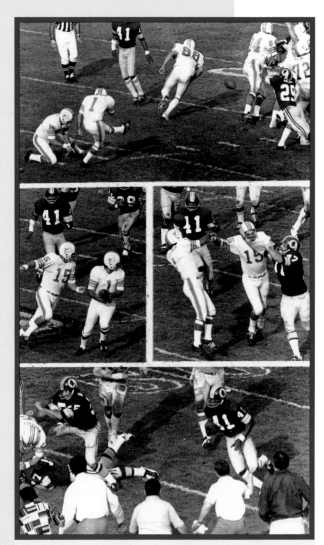

This sequence shows how a Dolphin field-goal attempt turned into a Redskin touchdown.

practiced. The football fluttered right into the hands of Mike Bass, who kept on running into the end zone.

With the score 14-7 and two minutes to go, the Redskins played magnificent defense and forced the Dolphins to punt. Kilmer would have one last chance to make something happen. The No-Names, however, made their presence felt one final time. They forced two incompletions, tackled Brown for a 4-yard loss, and then sacked Kilmer on fourth down to end the contest. The Dolphins were not perfect in Super Bowl VII, but with the win over the Redskins, their season was.

> **Dolphins 14**
> **Redskins 7**
> Best Player: Jake Scott

Super Bowl VIII
January 13, 1974
(1973 Season)
Minnesota Vikings (NFC)
vs. Miami Dolphins (AFC)

The Miami Dolphins became the first club to make it back to the Super Bowl for three consecutive years, this time with a 12-2 record. The Minnesota Vikings returned after a three-year absence with the same killer defense and an overhauled offense. Against any other team in football, the Vikings might have been favored, but Miami was at the peak of its powers as one of the greatest teams ever. Like the Redskins the year before, it looked as if Minnesota would need a lot of luck just to keep the score close.

No-Names no more, the stars of the Miami defense were now known to all football fans. Manny Fernandez, Bill Stanfill, Nick Buoniconti, Dick Anderson, and Jake Scott were selected as All Pros. In 1973, they allowed a league-low 150 points—less than 10 a game—and had an impenetrable pass defense. On offense, the Dolphins got great seasons from Larry Csonka, Mercury Morris, Paul Warfield, and Bob Griese again.

The Minnesota defense appeared to be up to the task of stopping this group. The front four—Alan Page, Carl Eller, Jim Marshall, and Gary Larsen—was in top form, while Paul Krause and Bobby Bryant shut down the right side of the field to enemy passing attacks. The big news for the Vikings was the return of their 1960s hero Fran Tarkenton and the eye-opening play of rookie Chuck Foreman. Tarkenton, older and wiser—and still an expert scrambler—brought to life the fluid offense that Coach Bud Grant had been developing over 15 seasons. Foreman, a first-round pick out of the University of Miami, challenged tacklers with a mix of raw power and spectacular agility. These two talents, working together for the first time, blended seamlessly to outscore opponents by 128 points.

After finishing 12-2 and rolling over the Redskins and the Cowboys during the regular season, the Vikings had every right to expect royal treatment when they arrived for the game in Houston. It must have been quite a shock when they entered their practice facilities in the Delmar School. Apparently, no one from the league had bothered to check it out before agreeing to use it. When the Vikings entered the locker room, they found something important was missing: lockers. Only 3 of the 15 shower heads actually produced water—and two were being used by nesting birds. "Men," announced team veteran Jim Marshall, "consider yourself honored. It is the first time we have ever showered in an aviary."

Things did not improve for Marshall & Co. once the game started. On the Dolphins' first drive, they bullied Minnesota all the way down the field, and Csonka scored on a 5-yard run. Six minutes later, Jim Kiick burrowed in from the 1-yard line to up the score to 14-0. Meanwhile, Tarkenton could get nowhere against Miami. Not until the end of the first quarter did he record Minnesota's first first down.

Minnesota's defense fared better in the second quarter, yielding only a field goal. And Tarkenton found some measure of success with about 5 minutes left in the half. He led a splendid drive from his own 20-yard line to the Miami 6, where the Vikings faced a fourth-and-one. Rather than settling for a field goal, Grant opted to go for the first down. He sent in a running play for Oscar Reed, who got the needed yardage but then fumbled. Scott fell on the ball to end the threat.

Down 17-0, Minnesota hoped to solve the Miami defense in the second half. Foreman had been unable to break free, and the Dolphins' disciplined zone had limited Tarkenton to short passes. Unless something changed, the Vikings would not make up 17 points.

Something did change, and it was the score. Starting a drive inside Minnesota territory, Griese connected with Warfield on a long pass, and then Csonka plunged into the end zone to make the score 24-0. Penalties and errors continued to plague the Vikings throughout the second half, keeping them from mounting a serious threat until late in the game.

Midway through the fourth quarter,

Larry Csonka takes a handoff from Bob Griese and prepares to bust through the Minnesota defense. Csonka gained 145 yards and scored a pair of touchdowns in a one-sided Miami victory.

Tarkenton took his team on a 57-yard drive, running the ball into the end zone himself. The Dolphins ended any fantasy of a comeback when they intercepted Tarkenton on Minnesota's next possession. Then Kiick and Csonka ran out the last 6 minutes to finish the game.

While most fans spent the winter debating whether or not the Dolphins were the

IRON CITY CENTERPIECE

Mike Webster played center for the Steelers for 17 years. He anchored an offensive line that helped the team win four Super Bowls.

The Pittsburgh Steelers of the 1970s were so loaded with All-Pros and Hall of Famers that many fans failed to appreciate a major reason for their success: the offensive line. These were the guys who gave quarterback Terry Bradshaw the time he needed to pick out receivers. They were also the ones who created holes for Franco Harris and Rocky Bleier, whose skill at following their blockers went largely unnoticed. The key man in Pittsburgh's front five was center Mike Webster, who ranks among the best ever to play the position.

At 6-foot-2 (1.88 m) and 250 pounds (113 kg), Webster was on the small side for a center, but many believed him to be the strongest man in the NFL. Webster made up for his lack of size by using his head—and then the rest of his body—to cut down the defensive tackles and middle linebackers who stormed his position on every play. He was also tough and durable. Webster once played an astonishing 177 games in a row.

Webster's intelligence is what ultimately set him apart from his peers. When the Steelers broke from their huddle, he would scan the defense and warn his linemates what was coming. Sometimes he turned to Bradshaw and suggested a new play as he lowered himself into his stance—which is something centers almost never do. Forgotten after his 17-year career ended, Webster drifted away from football and into poverty. When he was elected to the Hall of Fame in 1997, his story came to light, and a legion of his old fans and friends came to his aid.

The mastermind behind this group was coach Chuck Noll, a supreme strategist who cared about one thing only: winning championships. Noll preferred the conservative approach and rarely gambled on a big play. At the beginning of the year he benched Bradshaw, who had a habit of trying low-percentage passes. After winning back the job from Joe Gilliam, Bradshaw stayed within Noll's game plan, and the Steelers lost just one game the rest of the way.

The Vikings hoped Bradshaw would return to his old ways and attack them, but he did not. Fearful of each other's defense, both teams played timidly during the first half. Midway through the second period, the Vikings made a costly mistake. Tarkenton, working from deep in his own territory, botched a pitchout to Foreman. The veteran quarterback pounced on the ball but was tackled in his own end zone for a safety.

The Vikings blew another chance right before halftime, when Tarkenton hit John Gilliam with a pass at the Steeler 5-yard line. Safety Glen Edwards slammed into Gilliam, jarring the ball loose. Blount was on it in an instant to end the threat. The Steelers made mistakes, too. During the second quarter, they got within field-goal range, but both times they failed to convert. The score at halftime was 2-0, Pittsburgh.

Both teams felt good about their chances in the second half. The quickness of the Vikings had made Bradshaw jumpy and promised to create some turnovers during the final 30 minutes. The Steelers were pleased about their running attack. Although it had not produced a score, Noll felt his blockers had gained the upper hand on the Minnesota defense.

The Steelers kicked off to open the third quarter. Seconds later, the Vikings found themselves in an impossible situation. Return man Bill Brown—a rock of consistency with the team since 1962—fumbled the ball, and Marv Kellum recovered it for the Steelers on the 30-yard line. Franco Harris took over from there, scoring on a long run to make it 9-0.

The Vikings finally got on the scoreboard in the fourth quarter. With Pittsburgh punting from its own end zone, Blair crashed through the line and blocked the ball. Teammate Terry Brown recovered for a touchdown to make the score 9-6, but Fred Cox missed the extra point.

Now the Minnesota defense had to get the ball back. Starting on their own 34-yard line after Cox's kickoff, the Steelers pounded the ball right down the Vikings' throat. Time and again, Pittsburgh got the necessary first-down yardage it needed to keep the drive alive. With the ball on the 4-yard line, Bradshaw rolled out with his eye on the end zone. Paul Krause, a future Hall of Famer, had to decide whether to stay with his man—tight end Larry Brown—or veer toward Bradshaw, who had turned toward the goal line. Krause hesitated for just an instant, and Bradshaw gunned a pass right by him into Brown's arms for a touchdown.

Roy Gerela's kick made the score 16-6, and that is how the game ended. Harris, with 158 rushing yards, was voted MVP. The real star of the game, however, was the Pittsburgh defense, which had kept Tarkenton contained in the pocket and had limited Foreman to a mere 18 yards.

Steelers 16
Vikings 6
Best Player: Franco Harris

Super Bowl X
January 18, 1976
(1975 Season)
Dallas Cowboys (NFC)
vs. Pittsburgh Steelers (AFC)

Grit versus glamour. If ever there was a Super Bowl matchup that offered these two qualities, this was it. The Pittsburgh Steelers, specialists in smash-mouth football, were pitted against the squeaky-clean Dallas Cowboys, who would come to be known as "America's Team." For longtime football fans, this promised to be the best Super Bowl yet.

The Steelers, now experienced and confident, tore through the regular season with 11 straight wins to finish at 12-2. Pushed by the Houston Oilers and the Cincinnati Bengals (their much-improved division rivals), Pittsburgh played near-flawless football and rolled through the playoffs with ease. Once again, the dominant offensive line keyed the running and passing attacks. Franco Harris and Rocky Bleier combined for more than 1,750 yards, and Terry Bradshaw threw for 18 touchdowns. Lynn Swann, the silky-smooth second-year receiver, caught 11 of those scoring passes. The defense was amazing again despite injuries to Joe Greene.

Jack Ham (#59) wraps up a Dallas ball carrier with an assist from cornerback J.T. Thomas (#24). Ham was one of three great linebackers in Pittsburgh's "Steel Curtain" defense.

Monstrous Jack Lambert continued to improve, while the secondary—led by Mel Blount's 11 interceptions—picked off a total of 24 passes.

At the beginning of the Cowboys' season, many fans believed it would be a rebuilding year. The defense had grown old since its last appearance in the Super Bowl, with Pro Bowlers Bob Lilly, George Andrie, Pat Toomay, Chuck Howley, and Herb Adderley retiring. A group of splendid replacements slotted right in for coach Tom Landry, however, as youngsters Harvey Martin, Randy White, Thomas "Hollywood" Henderson, and Ed "Too Tall" Jones played like veterans in Landry's innovative "Flex" defense, which would tighten up or spread out depending on the situation.

The Dallas offense was now in the capable hands of Roger Staubach. His favorite receiver, Drew Pearson, accounted for eight touchdowns, while Robert Newhouse, Doug Dennison, and ex-Steeler Preston Pearson provided an ample running game. The Cowboy offense could pass right over you, run right through you, or fool you with a bag of trick plays.

The Cowboys snagged a Wild Card berth in the playoffs with a 10-4 record, then beat the Vikings on a last-second "hail-Mary" pass from Staubach to Pearson. In the NFC championship game, Dallas crushed the Los Angeles Rams, 37-7. No Wild Card had ever reached the big game before.

Flex or no flex, the Steelers planned to run the Cowboys into the ground. And that is just how the game began, as Harris carried the ball four times in five plays. That strategy changed, however, after Dallas got the ball deep in Pittsburgh territory when punter Bobby Walden fumbled the snap.

Staubach connected with Drew Pearson on a scoring strike, and just like that it was 7-0. Incredibly, it was the first first-quarter touchdown allowed by the Steelers all season long!

Bradshaw came right back with a long drive of his own. This time, he utilized the pass perfectly. He caught Dallas by surprise with a 32-yard pass to Swann, then crossed up the Cowboys again on third-and-one from the 7-yard line. With the defense bunched to stop Franco, Bradshaw flicked a pass to tight end Randy Grossman for an easy score. Dallas broke the tie with a field goal on the next drive. With less than a minute left, Pittsburgh kicker Roy Gerela missed a 36-yard field-goal try. The Cowboys took a 10-7 lead into the locker room at halftime.

The defensive battle continued in the third quarter, with neither club scoring. Gerela missed another chance to tie the game when his 33-yard kick drifted left. Pittsburgh narrowed the score to 10-9 early in the fourth quarter when Reggie Harrison blocked a Dallas punt for a safety. After receiving their free kick, the Steelers took the lead when Gerela finally split the uprights with a 36-yard field goal. Staubach added fuel to the fire when he threw an interception on Dallas's next possession. Mike Wagner returned the ball to the 7-yard line, and Gerela extended the Pittsburgh advantage to 15-10 with another field goal.

Cowboy fans did not panic. They knew that one touchdown would give them the lead again. That changed a few minutes later, though, when Bradshaw, reading a safety blitz perfectly, found Swann in single-man coverage and hit him for a 64-yard touchdown. Gerela's point-after attempt clanked against the post, but the Steelers

WRIGHT MAN, WRONG CHOICE

The play that swung the momentum from Dallas to Pittsburgh in the fourth quarter of Super Bowl X was Reggie Harrison's blocked punt. It not only produced a safety, but also led to a Roy Gerela field goal that gave the Steelers a 12-10 lead. How did Harrison, who had never blocked a punt in his entire life, get through so easily?

Ask Rayfield Wright.

No, he wasn't the one who let Harrison through. Still, he still feels at least partially responsible.

Before the play, the game was interrupted by Bambi Brown, a local dancer who ran on the field and handed Wright a silver horseshoe good-luck charm. As security guards escorted Brown to the sideline, Wright looked at the horseshoe and then flung it away. Moments later, the Cowboys' fortunes took a devastating turn for the worse.

"Maybe I should have hung on to it," said Wright.

---

were now in command at 21-10 with just 3 minutes left.

With Pittsburgh in a cautious "prevent" defense, Staubach went to work. He fired four terrific passes, and a minute later the Cowboys were in the end zone. Down 21-17, Dallas attempted to get the ball back with an onside kick. The Steelers saw it coming and recovered the ball on the 42-yard line. With 1 minute and 48 seconds left to play, the Cowboys needed to keep the Steelers from achieving a first down. Two runs by Harris and one by Bleier netted just 1 yard. The Cowboys called time-out after each play, which left plenty of time on the clock.

Coach Noll went against accepted wisdom and decided not to punt the ball. He preferred to let Staubach start his final drive 60 yards away than to risk a blocked punt. Bleier gained 2 yards on a run, and the Cowboys got the ball back. Staubach

sprinted for 11 yards and passed to Preston Pearson for another 12 to reach the Pittsburgh 38. The drive stalled there when Staubach threw a pair of incompletions before he was intercepted by Glen Edwards. It was an exciting finish to an excellent game.

> **Steelers 21**
> **Cowboys 17**
>   Best Player: Lynn Swann

Super Bowl XI
January 9, 1977
(1976 Season)
Minnesota Vikings (NFC)
vs. Oakland Raiders (AFC)

The swashbuckling Oakland Raiders got a second shot at the Super Bowl nine years after their first appearance, while the aging

Minnesota Vikings returned for a record fourth time. Each team had fooled a legion of doubters to advance to the ultimate game. Now the naysayers believed the Vikings would fall apart.

The Raiders, a rough-and-ready defensive club, looked dead in the preseason after three of their four starting defensive linemen were felled by injury. Coach John Madden switched to a 3-4 scheme, which relied heavily on the play of his linebackers. They did not disappoint him. Ted Hendricks, Phil Villapiano, Willie Hall, and Monte Johnson wreaked havoc on the enemy, while the Oakland offense rode the arm of quarterback Ken Stabler to an NFL-best 13 victories.

Still, all bets were on the Steelers in the AFC championship game. Pittsburgh had allowed just one touchdown in its final nine regular-season games and had killed the Colts in the first round of the playoffs. Injuries to Franco Harris and Rocky Bleier in that game opened the door for the Raiders, however. They slammed it on Bradshaw & Co. with a decisive 24-7 victory.

The Vikings still had the same core of defensive players that began the decade: Carl Eller, Alan Page, Jim Marshall, Paul Krause, and Bobby Bryant. Somehow, they turned back the clock. The Purple People Eaters allowed just 176 points in 14 games, and they were particularly tough on pass-oriented opponents. On offense, 36-year-old Fran Tarkenton was rejuvenated by young speedsters Sammy White and Ahmad Rashad, who combined for more than 100 catches. Anchoring the offense was Chuck Foreman, who scored 14 times and surpassed 1,700 total yards from scrimmage.

Both teams started Super Bowl XI nervously, as they felt each other out. The Raiders had the first scoring chance, but they came up empty when Errol Mann missed his field-goal attempt. A blocked punt gave the Vikings the game's next golden opportunity. They blew that, too, when Villapiano stripped the ball from Brent McClanahan on the 2-yard line and Hall recovered for Oakland.

Now Stabler went to work. Starting deep in Raider territory, he directed a 12-play, 90-yard drive that resulted in a field goal. On the next series, Stabler took the Raiders all the way, capping a ten-play drive with a short pass to tight end Dave Casper. Oakland's third score of the second period came on a run by Pete Banaszak after Neal Colzie made a great punt return. Mann missed the extra point, but the Raiders owned a commanding 16-0 lead at the half.

As the experts had predicted, the long season seemed to be taking its toll on the aged Viking defenders. Meanwhile, Oakland's linebackers were having no trouble stopping Tarkenton and Foreman. Madden told his players to keep the pressure on. Minnesota would have to start gambling soon, and this was not what Bud Grant's system was designed to do.

The Raiders increased their advantage to 19-0 on another Mann field goal, but the Vikings capitalized on two devastating penalties to put together a nifty touchdown drive. The score remained 19-7 as the game headed into the fourth quarter. Minnesota mounted a threat when Tarkenton moved the team to Oakland's 37-yard line. Then Hall, who already had a fumble recovery, intercepted a pass to take the air out of the Vikings.

Stabler finished the job with a beautiful 48-yard pass to veteran Fred Biletnikoff,

AL OR NOTHING

Oakland's first Super Bowl championship was especially sweet for team owner Al Davis, who delighted in stirring up trouble among football's more conservative owners. In 1963, at the age of 34, he was made head coach and general manager of the Raiders. Three years later, he was named commissioner of the American Football League.

Davis's first move as the AFL's top man was to launch an attack on the NFL by signing its best quarterbacks to lucrative future contracts. Afraid that Davis might be leading pro football toward financial ruin, owners in both leagues agreed to merge the AFL and the NFL. Davis was furious. He believed the AFL would have forced the NFL to its knees, thus making Davis the most powerful man in the game.

This began a long feud with NFL commissioner Pete Rozelle. Davis made a point of challenging Rozelle's decisions, and he successfully sued the NFL when his move to Los Angeles was blocked in 1980. Throughout the 1980s and 1990s and into the twenty-first century, Davis continued to be a thorn in the NFL's side.

Oakland captured its first title in Super Bowl XI under the guidance of coach John Madden (left). No one enjoyed this triumph more than team owner Al Davis (right), who had a long-running feud with NFL commissioner Pete Rozelle.

Fred Biletnikoff (left) celebrates with quarterback Ken Stabler (right). Biletnikoff was the game's MVP.

which set up Banaszak's second touchdown run of the day. All that remained for Tarkenton was to heave desperation passes. Cornerback Willie Brown—a starter in Oakland's Super Bowl II humiliation—finally tasted postseason glory when he stepped in front of White at the 25-yard line and grabbed a Tarkenton pass. Brown weaved his way to a spectacular 75-yard score.

With the count 32-7 and the game out of reach, an exhausted Tarkenton sat out Minnesota's final series. Backup David Lee passed the Vikings to a touchdown, but it was too little, too late. The mighty Vikings—one of the best teams in history—had lost their fourth Super Bowl in eight years.

> **Raiders 32**
> **Vikings 14**
>   Best Player: Fred Biletnikoff

Super Bowl XII
January 15, 1978
(1977 Season)
Dallas Cowboys (NFC)
vs. Denver Broncos (AFC)

From 1969 to 1973, Craig Morton rarely went a day without wondering when Heisman Trophy winner Roger Staubach would come in and take his starting job. Belittled for most of his career as a Cowboy, Morton nonetheless led Dallas to three straight division titles. After being exiled to the pitiful Giants in a 1974 trade, he resurfaced with the Denver Broncos in 1977 and led them all the way to the AFC championship. With the Cowboys winning the NFC title, Super Bowl XII had all the makings of an Old West shoot-out.

For the Cowboys to hit their target, they needed rookie star Tony Dorsett to continue his great season. The Cowboys' first Hall-of-Fame caliber runner, he topped 1,000 yards and scored 13 touchdowns. With defenses worrying about Dorsett, Staubach had more freedom than ever to connect with Drew Pearson, who led all of football with 870 receiving yards. The Dallas defense continued to dominate as its young stars matured and replaced the familiar faces of old. Coach Tom Landry's lone adjustment was to move linebacker Randy White up to the line. The guy they called the "Man-ster" used his quickness to become the top all-around defensive tackle in the league.

The Broncos' chief gunslinger may have been Morton, but Denver did the most damage with its defense. Coach Red Miller, in his first year, encouraged a gambling style of play that made the most of hard-hitters Lyle Alzado, Rubin Carter, Randy Gradishar, and Tom Jackson. Their "Orange

Crush" defense was a twist on John Madden's 3-4, and soon its focal point—the "nose tackle"—became the most talked-about position in football. Neither the Steelers nor the Raiders (both big favorites) was able to beat Denver in the playoffs, but the Cowboys seemed built for the task. The two teams matched up extremely well on both sides of the ball.

The first Super Bowl ever played indoors (in the Louisiana Superdome) began unexpectedly. In the opening moments of the first quarter, the Cowboys bobbled a tricky double-reverse, dropped a punt, and fumbled a handoff. Each time they recovered the ball and dodged disaster. It was just a few minutes into the game, and Bronco fans could not help but wonder if their best chance at victory had already passed them by.

Their fears were confirmed when Morton, under a heavy rush from White and Harvey Martin, threw a weak pass that was caught by Dallas safety Randy Hughes. Dorsett banged in from the 3-yard line a few

plays later to give the Cowboys a 7-0 lead. The Broncos found themselves down 10-0 after Morton threw a second interception on Denver's next possession and Dallas kicker Efram Herrera kicked a 35-yard field goal.

Clearly rattled, the Broncos came unglued in the second quarter. Morton was intercepted again, and Denver ball carriers fumbled three times. Thank goodness for the Orange Crush, which limited Staubach to a mere field goal. The half ended 13-0, with Denver fans heaving a sigh of relief. Could their team play any worse? It seemed impossible. Perhaps the second half would bring a reversal of fortune.

Coach Miller was not so optimistic. He informed Morton that he would pull him from the game if he continued to mess up. In the opposing locker room, Coach Landry had no plans to remove Staubach. Still, he let his offense know that he expected much better play in the second half.

The Broncos began the third quarter with the ball, and Morton moved them into

Despite a broken right thumb, Dallas receiver Butch Johnson was able to cradle this long pass from Roger Staubach. His touchdown gave the Cowboys a commanding lead in Super Bowl XII.

A STICKY SITUATION

Robert Newhouse was the perfect man to execute a surprise touchdown throw. No one on the Cowboys looked less like a passer. Newhouse stood at 5-foot-9 (1.9 m) and weighed 220 pounds (113 kg); his thighs were so enormous that he had to have his pants specially tailored. Whenever he got the ball, defensive players prepared themselves for a low-to-the-ground collision. Knowing this, Coach Tom Landry had Newhouse practice his passing all week long.

Once the game started, Newhouse forgot about the play. As usual, he coated his hands with Stickum, a tacky substance used to prevent fumbles. When Roger Staubach called the option pass in the huddle, Newhouse's spine went cold. He began wiping his hands on his pants furiously, but then got even more scared when he realized he might be tipping off the Broncos. Luckily, Denver never noticed, and Newhouse completed a spectacular (and slightly sticky) touchdown pass to Golden Richards.

Dallas fullback Robert Newhouse (#44) launches a pass downfield in a surprise play against the Denver Broncos. Despite a handful of Stickum, Newhouse led Golden Richards perfectly.

field-goal range. Jim Turner, kicking hero of Super Bowl III, blasted the ball through the uprights from 47 yards away, and the Broncos were on the scoreboard. Dallas countered later in the quarter. After advancing the ball across midfield, the Cowboys faced a third-and-10 from Denver's 45-yard line. Rather than going for the first down, Staubach launched a high, arcing 50-yard pass. Wideout Butch Johnson, playing tight end because of a broken thumb, was the surprise target. He snared it with his fingertips and crossed the goal line in midair. The ball popped loose when Johnson slammed to the artificial turf, but the official signaled that he had maintained possession long enough for the play to count. Dallas now enjoyed a 20-3 lead.

The never-say-die Broncos came right back with a 67-yard kickoff return by Rick Upchurch. On the next play, Morton threw a ball right into the hands of Dallas star Too Tall Jones, who dropped it. Miller had seen enough. Morton was summoned to the bench, and backup Norris Weese entered the game. Four plays later, Rob Lytle plowed into the end zone to bring the Broncos within ten points again.

Dallas did not consider its lead very secure. Dorsett had injured his knee, and Staubach had broken a finger on his throwing hand. The aggressive Denver defense was smelling blood. Landry assessed the situation and decided to use the Broncos' aggressiveness against them. Staubach pitched out to fullback Robert Newhouse, who headed for the right side. Just as a group of Denver defenders turned to meet him, Newhouse floated a pass to Golden Richards, who was open. Richards made a marvelous diving catch in the end zone for a touchdown.

That was the end of the scoring. The Denver Broncos, 27-10 losers, were humiliated. The bruised and battered Cowboys, Super Bowl champions for the second time, felt like they needed a long vacation. Staubach, who went 17-for-25 and threw for 183 yards, was named MVP. Morton, a measly 4-for-15, threw half as many interceptions in the first half as he had during the entire regular season.

> **Cowboys 27**
> **Broncos 10**
> Best Players: Randy White
>   and Harvey Martin

Super Bowl XIII
January 21, 1979
(1978 Season)
Dallas Cowboys (NFC)
vs. Pittsburgh Steelers (AFC)

The last Super Bowl of the 1970s would decide the "Team of the 70s"—the unofficial title to which both the Pittsburgh Steelers and the Dallas Cowboys aspired. Both clubs were at the height of their fame and the peak of their powers. A record number of viewers tuned in to watch a game that they expected to be nothing short of fantastic.

After stumbling through the early part of their season, the Dallas Cowboys came together nicely and won their final six games. All but one starter returned to the defense, and the offense was bolstered by a great second year from Tony Dorsett, as well as a new rule that helped receivers. Previously, defenders could smack receivers around anywhere on the field until the ball was thrown. In 1978, the area of contact was limited to 5 yards off the line of scrimmage. This lent a whole new dimension to the games of Drew Pearson and rookie Tony Hill, who were free to run their routes almost untouched.

The NFL's tight ends also benefited from this rule. Dallas's Billy Joe DuPree caught 34 balls and scored 9 touchdowns. With defensive secondaries playing more cautiously, running backs also had more room to operate on short passes. Roger Staubach exploited this opportunity and connected with Dorsett, Preston Pearson, and Robert Newhouse more than 100 times.

The Steelers also took advantage of the new rule. Terry Bradshaw, who was now in his prime as a passer, threw for 28 touchdowns and transformed the Pittsburgh offense into an unstoppable monster. His favorite targets, Lynn Swann and John Stallworth, caught 102 balls and scored 20 times. With opponents fearing Bradshaw's arm, the legs of Franco Harris and Rocky Bleier were more productive than ever. The duo averaged 120 yards and a touchdown per game. As for the Steeler defense, it gave up less than 200 points in a year when most teams allowed 300 to 400. Seven of its eleven starters—including defensive backs Mel Blount, Mike Wagner, and Donnie Shell—made All-Pro.

Would this game be a defensive war or an offensive exhibition? It was impossible to tell. Dallas opened the game by driving to the Pittsburgh 35-yard line, but a razzle-dazzle play backfired, and the Steelers gained possession of the football. Six plays later, Bradshaw connected with Stallworth in the end zone for a 28-yard touchdown and a 7-0 lead. Later in the first quarter, Harvey Martin sacked Bradshaw, knocking the ball loose. Too Tall Jones pounced on

By Super Bowl XIII, Terry Bradshaw of the Pittsburgh Steelers had matured into a patient and intelligent passer.

THE DROP HEARD 'ROUND THE WORLD

The most-remembered moment of Super Bowl XIII is one that Hall of Famer Jackie Smith would rather forget. When the Dallas tight end dropped a certain touchdown pass from Roger Staubach, the Cowboys had to settle for a field goal.

The Super Bowl has the power to turn a benchwarmer into a national celebrity. It also can leave a permanent stain on a great player's career. To this day, Jackie Smith is remembered by millions of fans as the man who muffed the pass that lost the Super Bowl for the Cowboys.

The sad thing is that this is not entirely true. The fact is, Smith dropped a ball that would have tied the game in the third quarter. Also, he only cost his team four points, as Dallas kicked a field goal on the next play. Because of the drop, however, many forget that Smith was one of the greatest tight ends in the history of the game.

Playing in an era when his position was still developing, Smith put up numbers that any modern-day tight end would be proud of. In a dozen years as a starter, he caught more than 450 passes and scored 37 touchdowns. Smith was big and tough enough to snag balls over the

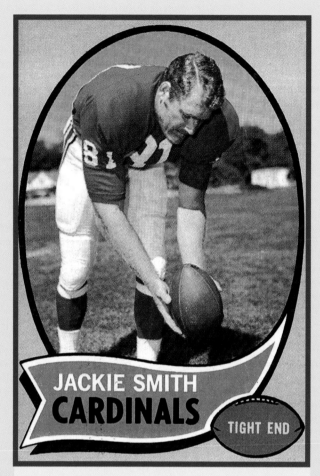

As this trading card shows, Jackie Smith was famous for his "great hands" when he was with the Cardinals. He was voted All-NFL each year from 1966 to 1970.

middle, and also speedy enough to catch bombs. He was a good blocker and a fearless competitor rated as an equal to Mike Ditka and Tom Mackey, the other great tight ends of his generation. Those who saw Smith play during his prime years agree: no one ever had surer hands than old number 81.

Ironically, Smith had already retired when Tom Landry asked him if he would be willing to play one more season as a backup for starter Billy Jo Dupree. In 15 years with the St. Louis Cardinals, Smith had never made it to the postseason, so he agreed. In the weeks leading up to the Super Bowl, Smith acted like a kid in a candy store. He could hardly wait for the game to begin. Sadly, his moment of glory turned sour at the worst possible moment.

the fumble, and within minutes the Cowboys had tied the score on a Staubach-to-Hill touchdown pass.

By the second quarter, the pattern of the game seemed to be clear. Each offense was good enough to score on the opposing defense, but each defense was good enough to make the opposing offense pay dearly for even the slightest mistake. This was underscored when Bradshaw hung in the pocket too long and was stripped of the ball by Hollywood Henderson. Linebacker Mike Hegman scooped it up and returned it for a touchdown to put Dallas up 14-7.

The Steelers knotted the score on a defensive mistake. Bradshaw threw a 10-yard completion to Stallworth, and cornerback Aaron Kyle missed the tackle. Stallworth whirled around to see no one between him and the goal line. The fleet-footed receiver outraced the entire Dallas team 65 yards to the end zone. Pittsburgh took the lead after Blount, who was inexplicably playing out of position, turned out to be in the perfect place to intercept a Staubach pass. Working quickly, Bradshaw beat the clock with a 7-yard touchdown throw to Bleier right before the half.

Although Staubach was kicking himself for Blount's interception, the overall mood in the Dallas locker room was good. Limit mistakes, the Cowboys told one another, and they would win the game. Of course, the same things were being said in the Pittsburgh clubhouse. Both teams took the field for the third quarter and followed their own advice. The defenses were nearly flawless. The lone score in the period was a short field goal by the Cowboys. It followed a muffed pass in the end zone by veteran Jackie Smith that would have tied the score.

This mistake would turn out to be costly, as the Steeler offense suddenly came back to life. Pittsburgh scored again, with help from the officials. With the ball on his own 44-yard line, Bradshaw spotted a safety blitz coming and quickly unloaded the ball in the general direction of Swann. Cornerback Benny Barnes played Swann perfectly, making him run around him just to get near the pass. Swann tripped as he attempted this maneuver, but a flag was thrown on Barnes for interference. From there, Harris reached the end zone on a 22-yard scamper to give the Steelers a 28-17 lead.

The Steelers got another break on the ensuing kickoff, when Roy Gerela kicked the ball short by mistake. It went right to Randy White, who was caught by surprise and fumbled when he was hit by special-teams demon Tony Dungy. Dennis Winston recovered, and the Steelers scored soon after on an 18-yard touchdown pass from Bradshaw to Swann.

With a chance at victory all but gone, it was time for Staubach to remind fans why he was the comeback king of the 1970s. In no time, he moved the team deep into Steeler territory from his own 11-yard line. He connected with DuPree for a 7-yard touchdown to make the score 35-24 with less than 3 minutes left. The expected on-side kick went to Dungy, who erased his earlier good play by fumbling the football. Dallas recovered and exploded for another score to make it 35-31.

This time, Rafael Septien's onside kick went to Rocky Bleier, one of the most reliable Steelers. Bleier got a kind bounce and fell to the ground. Short of time-outs, the helpless Cowboys watched the clock tick away as Bradshaw kneeled on two snaps to end the game. Was the Team of the 1970s question settled by the score? Perhaps. But the difference between the Super Bowl champion and the runner-up on this day was little more than a mistake or two and a lucky bounce.

Steelers 35
Cowboys 31
Best Player: Terry Bradshaw

CHAPTER 3

THE 1980s

Super Bowl XIV
January 20, 1980
(1979 Season)
Los Angeles Rams (NFC)
vs. Pittsburgh Steelers (AFC)

Throughout the 1970s, the class of the NFC West had been the Los Angeles Rams. Year in and year out they made the playoffs, but not once did the Rams advance to the Super Bowl. In 1979, Los Angeles had one of its worst seasons, posting a lackluster 9-7 record—and, of course, this was the year the Rams went all the way. In Super Bowl XIV, they faced the mighty Steelers, who were solid favorites.

Although they had to hold off a strong challenge from the Houston Oilers, Pittsburgh still had a very strong team. All the familiar names were still wearing the yellow and black. Terry Bradshaw threw for 3,724 yards and 26 touchdowns; Franco Harris ran for 1,186 yards and scored 12 times; and John Stallworth had a monster year, with 70 catches for 1,183 yards. The defense still had six players on the All-Pro squad, although it lacked the depth that it had previously enjoyed. Above all, the Steelers knew how to win the big game.

Chuck Noll did not take the Rams lightly. Unlike the Steelers, Los Angeles did have a deep roster. That saved them when the injury bug began to bite. The Rams lost several key players, including their quarterback, Pat Haden, and entered the 12th week of the season with a losing record. Young Vince Ferragamo, who had attempted just 35 passes in two years, stepped in and lost just one game in the rest of the season. The Rams did most of their damage on the ground, with Cullen Bryant and Wendell Tyler in the starring roles. But Ferragamo's strong arm gave the team something Haden had not: the threat of the bomb. The Los Angeles defense was superb. Fred Dryer, Jack Youngblood, Rod Perry, Nolan Cromwell, and "Hacksaw" Reynolds (who had once sawed a car in half) were the team's marquee players.

The Super Bowl started on a predictable note. Pittsburgh's "Steel Curtain" defense forced Los Angeles to punt on its first possession. Bradshaw then led a time-consuming, 11-play drive that produced a field goal by rookie Matt Bahr. To their credit, the Rams barely blinked. They got the ball in good position; Tyler made a 39-yard run; and a few minutes later, Bryant finished off the drive with a 1-yard touchdown plunge.

After a 45-yard kickoff return by Larry Anderson, the Steelers regained the lead 10-7 on a touchdown run by Harris. Coach Ray Malavasi made some subtle adjustments, and his defense kept Pittsburgh bottled up for the rest of the half. Meanwhile, the Los Angeles offense produced a pair of field goals by Pat Corrall. To the amazement of millions, the Rams jogged off the field at halftime with a 13-10 lead.

Noll told his players not to worry. There was nothing fancy about the L.A. offense, and the defense was good but not great. The Steelers just needed to play better.

The Rams had the momentum as the third quarter began. On Pittsburgh's first possession, however, Bradshaw hit Lynn Swann with a long touchdown pass. Cromwell had the interception all lined up, but he misjudged his jump. This turn of events did little to dim L.A.'s enthusiasm. They struck right back, regaining the lead with a touchdown of their own. After Ferragamo and Billy Waddy connected on a 50-yard pass, veteran halfback Lawrence McCutcheon stunned the Steelers when he pulled up and threw a 22-yard touchdown pass to Ron Smith. Corrall missed the kick, but the Rams were now ahead 19-17. A major upset appeared to be in the making.

Few receivers in football history were as graceful or electrifying as Pittsburgh's Lynn Swann. He gave the Rams fits in Super Bowl XIV.

Though Terry Bradshaw earned MVP honors in Super Bowl XIV, many fans believed linebacker Jack Lambert (#58) deserved the award. He disrupted the Los Angeles offense throughout the game.

Bradshaw, trying to force the action, threw two interceptions. Still, as the game entered the fourth quarter, the Steelers remained calm. Three minutes into the period, Bradshaw found the end zone. He spotted Stallworth streaking down the field and threw a perfect spiral that hit the lanky wide receiver in stride. The 73-yard touchdown put Pittsburgh back in front, 24-19.

Once again, Ferragamo was able to move the Rams into Pittsburgh territory. This time his inexperience betrayed him, however. Ferragamo called a play-action pass, which is meant to "freeze" the linebackers and create better passing lanes.

JACK IS WILD

By the time Terry Bradshaw achieved his fourth Super Bowl victory, Pittsburgh fans had come to adore him. Still, they had to wonder why he was voted MVP of Super Bowl XIV. The heart and soul of the Steelers on this day was linebacker Jack Lambert, who was in on 13 tackles and made a key fourth-quarter interception.

Lambert's contribution in this game went beyond mere statistics. Late in the first half, after Los Angeles had scored three times, he gathered his troops and howled at them with such ferocity that several players admitted they were more scared of "Jack the Ripper" than they were of the Rams. In the second half, the Steelers slammed the lid on Los Angeles and allowed just six more points the rest of the way.

This performance was typical of Lambert, whose reputation for toughness was exceeded only by his actual toughness. Too tall, too skinny and—some say—too angry to be as good a linebacker as he was, Lambert made up for his shortcomings with an ability to read and react quickly to developing plays. He could chase fleet-footed halfbacks from sideline to sideline, stop burly fullbacks dead in their tracks, and separate quarterbacks from their senses with his lightning-quick blitzes.

For nine straight years Lambert was voted to the Pro Bowl—an amazing accomplishment. When he retired, many believed him to be the finest middle linebacker in history. Lambert could match such legends as Sam Huff, Joe Schmidt, Ray Nitschke, and Dick Butkus in every phase of the game. In one area he surpassed them all: He was so good on passing downs that opponents were forced to view him as a fifth defensive back.

The do-everything linebacker even amazed his fellow Steelers at times. "Jack has a role on this team," Mean Joe Greene once told a reporter. "I can't tell you what the role is, but he plays it very well!"

Jack Lambert—who was all over the field making great tackles—was not fooled. Ferragamo attempted to throw to Smith, but Lambert beat him to the pass and made the interception.

Bradshaw finished off the Rams right away. For the second time, he and Stallworth beat Perry deep, this time for 45 yards. An interference call gave the Steelers the ball on the Rams' 1-yard line, and Harris scored on Pittsburgh's third attempt to ram it in. With less than 2 minutes remaining, there was nothing the Rams could do. The Steelers had their fourth Super Bowl victory, 31-19.

Were the Rams that good, or was the

Steeler dynasty coming to an end? The debate still rages. The Steelers would not return to the Super Bowl until the 1990s. The Rams did not even win their division the following year.

> **Steelers 31**
> **Rams 19**
>   Best Player: Terry Bradshaw

Super Bowl XV
January 25, 1981
(1980 Season)
Philadelphia Eagles (NFC)
vs. Oakland Raiders (AFC)

Prior to 1980, the formula for building a Super Bowl team involved a lot of time and plenty of homegrown talent. The Oakland Raiders changed all that. Only a handful of players remained from their last Super Bowl squad, and many of the key contributors were brand new to the team. The Philadelphia Eagles got to the big game the old-fashioned way, improving year by year and maturing together before they made the big leap.

The two combatants in Super Bowl XV were different in other ways. The Eagles were a dull, defense-oriented team driven by an intense young coach named Dick Vermeil. Grizzled and ancient middle linebacker Bill Bergey was Philadelphia's emotional leader, along with veteran linemen Carl Hairston and Charles Johnson. Randy Logan and Herman Edwards handled matters in the secondary. The Eagle offense was powered by oft-injured Wilbert Montgomery. When healthy, he was one of the finest runners who ever played. Ex-Ram

Ron Jaworski, who had watched his former NFL team reach the Super Bowl the previous winter, became the toast of Philadelphia with 27 touchdowns and more than 3,500 passing yards.

The Raiders were far more adventurous. Owner Al Davis, who loved to tweak the league's nose, encouraged his players to cultivate a renegade image. Many had been banished from other teams, including former Heisman Trophy winner Jim Plunkett.

Oakland linebacker Rod Martin waves to the fans after Super Bowl XV. His interception in the first quarter set the tone for the game.

After throwing just 15 passes in two years as a bench player, Plunkett was thrust into the starting role when top gun Dan Pastorini broke his leg. Mixing passes to old-timers Bob Chandler, Ray Chester, and Cliff Branch, the 32-year-old Plunkett guided Oakland to a Wild Card berth. Art Shell and Gene Upshaw still anchored the offense, which punched holes for runners Mark Van Eeghan and Kenny King. The Oakland defense featured a group of fun-loving hard hitters, including noted eccentrics John Matuszak, Ted Hendricks, Matt Millen, and Lester Hayes. They confused and frightened opponents with their wildness, but when they needed to make a big play, they became deadly serious.

For the first time in Super Bowl history, the game featured two teams that had played each other earlier in the year. Philadelphia had beaten Oakland 10-7 in the season's 12th game, and thus was given a slight edge in this meeting. That edge disappeared on the Eagles' first series, however, when Raider linebacker Rod Martin intercepted Jaworski at midfield and returned it to the 30-yard line. Plunkett trotted on the field and, with the aid of an ill-timed penalty on the Eagles, got Oakland to the Philadelphia 2-yard line. He found Branch alone in the end zone on third down, and ex-Pittsburgh kicker Matt Bahr converted the extra point for a 7-0 lead. Two possessions later, Jaworski took to the air again and hit Rodney Parker with a nice throw for a 40-yard touchdown. But the other wideout, Harold Carmichael, had been flagged for illegal motion. The play was called back, and the Eagles failed to score.

Plunkett produced the play of the game on Oakland's next series. Under a heavy rush, the veteran heaved a desperation pass meant for King, and Edwards moved in to intercept it. Somehow it went right through his arms, and King found himself with clear sailing to the goal line, some 60 yards away. The 80-yard touchdown put the Raiders up 14-0. The Eagles managed a second-period field goal by barefoot kicker Tony Franklin, and that ended the scoring for the half.

In the locker room, Oakland coach Tom Flores saw no reason to alter his game plan, and he told his players as much. Vermeil tried to convince his players that their game plan was working, too. Erase a few uncharacteristic mistakes, he explained, and the Eagles might be up 13-0 instead of down 14-3.

There was no mistaking what happened in the second half, though. The Raiders took the game to the Eagles, and the Eagles folded. On the first drive of the second half, Plunkett picked the Philadelphia defense apart. He went 76 yards in 6 plays for the team's third touchdown, a 29-yard pass that Branch tore away from the hands of defender Roynell Young. Oakland increased its lead to 24-3 later in the third quarter on a 46-yard field goal by Bahr.

Jaworski battled back again, leading the Eagles on an 88-yard touchdown drive to cut the score to 24-10, but the Raiders were relentless. They ate up precious time with a 72-yard drive that produced another field goal. With less than 3 minutes left, Jaworski rushed the ball down the field. Once again, Martin was in the right place at the right time, and he picked off his third pass of the day to seal Philadelphia's fate.

Raiders 27
Eagles 10
Best Player: Jim Plunkett

DON'T GET TOO COMFORTABLE, JIM

After bouncing around the NFL for several seasons, Jim Plunkett found a home with the Raiders. He did not possess superstar skills, but he was a winner. And that is all that mattered in the Oakland organization.

The ups and downs of pro football are amazing sometimes. No one is a better example of this than Jim Plunkett. In college, he won the 1970 Heisman Trophy and restored Stanford University football to national prominence. Then Plunkett was the first player selected in the NFL draft. Following a fantastic rookie season with the New England Patriots, he seemed to have the football world at his feet.

After that, however, everything went downhill. Poor pass protection, a bad relationship with his coach, and a string of nagging injuries led to Plunkett's being benched in 1975, traded in 1976, and released in 1978. He joined the Oakland Raiders in 1979 and served as a backup to Ken Stabler. He threw a grand total of 15 passes that season. When the Raiders traded Stabler to Houston for first-stringer Dan Pastorini, they could not have sent Plunkett a clearer message. In their eyes, his days as an NFL starter were through.

Still, the Raiders were happy to have Plunkett, especially when Pastorini broke his leg in the fifth game of the season. With a record of 2-3, a second-string quarterback at the helm, and a lot of new faces on the roster, Oakland figured to win only four or five more games. Plunkett had watched his teammates from the sidelines for two years, however, and believed he knew how to whip them into winners. In his first game as a starter since 1977, he led Oakland to a 38-24 thrashing of the division-leading San Diego Chargers. The following week, Plunkett shocked the mighty Steelers 45-34.

By season's end, the Raiders had an 11-5 record and made the playoffs as a Wild Card. In the first round, Plunkett survived a brutal matchup with Stabler and the Oilers to win 27-7. In the second round, he engineered a fourth-quarter comeback to beat the Browns 14-12 in bone-chilling weather. In the AFC title game, Plunkett exploded for four first-half touchdowns, and Oakland held on to beat Dan Fouts and the Chargers 34-27. The Raiders were the first AFC Wild Card team ever to reach the Super Bowl. Plunkett, his career resurrected and his confidence restored, led the Raiders to a rousing win over the Philadelphia Eagles to complete his amazing year.

Relegated to bench duty once again in 1981, Plunkett won back his job in 1982 and delivered a division title. He lost the job again in 1983, only to be thrust back into the starting role when Marc Wilson hurt his shoulder late in the year. Once again, Plunkett led the Raiders through the playoffs, and he won a second Super Bowl.

Super Bowl XVI
January 24, 1982
(1981 Season)
San Francisco 49ers (NFC)
vs. Cincinnati Bengals (AFC)

In 1979, Bill Walsh was hired to coach the San Francisco 49ers. The team's prize draft pick, Notre Dame quarterback Joe Montana, watched from the bench as the team went 2-14. Two years later, after a 13-3 season, the 49ers were in the Super Bowl. Montana was the league's top-ranked passer, and Walsh was being hailed as a genius. "Who are these guys?" the world wondered. The same could be said of the AFC's team in Super Bowl XVI. The Cincinnati Bengals, in last place the season before, dominated the AFC. Before the season started, not a single football forecaster picked either of these clubs to make it to the big game. Few predicted they would even have winning records!

Actually, the Bengals owed much of their success to Walsh's genius, too. While serving as an assistant in Cincinnati during the 1970s, Walsh worked with quarterback Ken Anderson to make him one of the most accurate and intelligent quarterbacks in history. In 1981, Anderson connected for 29 touchdowns and completed a league-high 63 percent of his passes. His receiving corps included all-time great Isaac Curtis, rookie star Cris Collinsworth, and tight end Dan Ross. Anderson also threw to his backfield mates, including 1,000-yard man Pete Johnson, who snared 46 passes and scored a total of 16 touchdowns. The Bengal defense was anchored by end Ross Browner and cornerback Louis Breeden. Coach Forrest Gregg, a Hall of Fame lineman from the old Green Bay Packers, was smart, tough, and detail oriented.

The 49ers were a team built largely through Walsh's drafts, trades, and free-agent signings. Besides Montana, he added cornerbacks Ronnie Lott and Eric Wright; safeties Dwight Hicks and Carlton Williamson; defensive end Fred Dean; linebackers Hacksaw Reynolds and Keena Turner; runners Ricky Patton, Earl Cooper, and Johnny Davis; and receivers Charlie Young and Dwight Clark. It was Montana's

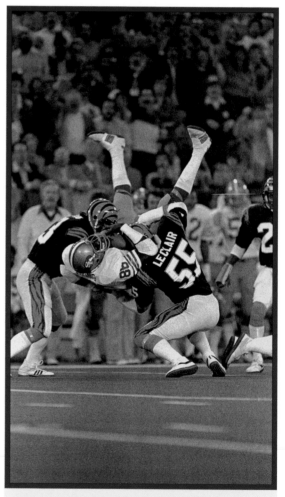

Cincinnati linebacker Jim LeClair brings down Charlie Young of the 49ers. San Francisco prevailed in a tight defensive battle, 26-21.

marvelous "no-look" throw to his buddy Clark in the back of the end zone that beat the Dallas Cowboys in the NFC championship game. This play signaled a changing of the guard in the conference, as the Cowboys began their long and distressing tumble from the top.

With so many unfamiliar faces, the pregame hype focused on the coaches and quarterbacks. Walsh and Gregg were heralded as the new-wave coaches. They blended crisp fundamentals like blocking and tackling with a more studious approach to the game. Each was imaginative and flexible when it came to devising his game plan, and neither was afraid to try new things if the old things were not working. Gregg was more of a taskmaster, like his old coach, Vince Lombardi. Walsh was soft-spoken, but he never failed to get his point across.

The quarterbacks were similar in style but different in approach. While both saw and understood the field as well as any passer in the game, Anderson was more conservative and patient in his attack. Montana liked to improvise, and he relished the opportunity to stage a dramatic comeback. The skinny young scrambler liked to create havoc, and he was confident in his ability to play well in tense situations.

With the whole world expecting a tight, crisply played contest, the game opened with a pair of bone-headed plays. The first came on the opening kickoff, when Amos Lawrence lost the ball for the 49ers. The Bengals soon returned the favor, as Anderson threw an interception at the goal line.

Things settled down quickly after that. Montana, moving his team with authority, went 68 yards for a touchdown. He did the honors himself with a 1-yard dive into the end zone. Ray Wersching booted the point-after for a 7-0 lead. The Bengals threatened on their first series of the second quarter but were thwarted once again by the San Francisco secondary. Throwing from the 27-yard line, Anderson hit Collinsworth with a pass, but Collinsworth fumbled the ball after taking a hit from Wright. The 49ers recovered the football, and once again Montana made Cincinnati pay for a crucial turnover. He went 92 yards in 12 plays for the game's second score, finishing with a short pass to Cooper for a 14-0 lead.

The 49ers struck again with a field goal with 18 seconds left in the half. Bengals special-teams star Archie Griffin—history's only two-time Heisman Trophy winner—failed to handle the ensuing kickoff and then compounded his brain-freeze by forgetting to go get the ball. Milt McColl downed it on the 4-yard line with enough time left for Wersching to kick another field goal. The 49ers went into the locker room up 20-0 and feeling pretty good.

Four Cincinnati mistakes had led directly to 20 San Francisco points. There was not much more analysis Gregg could do for his disappointed players. There was a silver lining in this dark cloud, however: It happened that the team had erased a 21-0 deficit in the season opener against the Seahawks. Gregg reminded his men that all they had done to win that game was to play as well as they could. He promised them that if they did the same against the 49ers, they would have a chance.

The Bengals opened the third quarter looking like a different team. Anderson orchestrated a 10-play march that covered 83 yards. At the 5-yard line, the quarterback took matters into his own hands and raced in for a score. Midway through the period,

NO-NONSENSE 'NINER

The key to San Francisco's victory in Super Bowl XVI was its remarkable goal-line stand in the third quarter. The play everyone remembers is Pete Johnson's unsuccessful attempt to score on fourth-and-one, when the entire 49ers defense seemed to hit him at once. Just as remarkable—and perhaps even more important—was the play made by linebacker Dan Bunz one down earlier.

Ken Anderson hit Charles Alexander with a short pass, and he looked like he would make the end zone with ease. Bunz closed in quickly, however, and grabbed the 6-foot-1 (1.85-m), 225-pound (102-kg) back by the waist an instant before he broke the plane of the goal line. Bunz, who was the same height and weight as Alexander, summoned a physics-defying burst of strength and threw Alexander backwards to prevent a score. Had Bunz tried any other type of tackle, Alexander would have dragged him into the end zone . . . and the game might have turned out very differently.

Anderson connected with Collinsworth for a first down on third-and-23, and this sent San Francisco reeling. Cincinnati pushed deep into San Francisco territory and ended up with a fourth-and-goal on the 1-yard line. Gregg decided to pass up a guaranteed field goal for the chance at a touchdown. Anderson handed off to Johnson, who was met by the entire 49ers team before he could cross the goal line. On this ill-fated drive, the Bengals ran eight plays from inside the 15-yard line and failed to reach the end zone.

The Cincinnati defense played a spectacular second half. Play after play, they made hard, punishing tackles. By the middle of the fourth quarter, Montana & Co. were looking thoroughly tenderized. The Bengals got their next scoring chance early in the fourth quarter, and Anderson made good on this one, hitting Dan Ross with a short pass to make the score 20-14. The 49ers, now less than a touchdown ahead, put together a long, time-consuming drive. The Bengals kept Montana out of the end zone, but the 49ers upped their lead to 23-14 on Wersching's third field goal.

Any hope the Bengals had disappeared when Anderson was intercepted by Wright. Montana burned up a few more minutes before Wersching connected on his fourth field goal to make the score 26-14. The 49ers, playing back to prevent a long scoring pass, let Anderson pass down the field for a touchdown to make the final score 26-21.

49ers 26
Bengals 21
        Best Player: Joe Montana

Super Bowl XVII
January 30, 1983
(1982 Season)
Washington Redskins (NFC)
vs. Miami Dolphins (AFC)

For the second year in a row, neither of the Super Bowl teams had been expected to make the playoffs when the season started. This was not a normal year, however. Two weeks into the season, the players staged a strike. By the time it was settled in November, there were only seven games left to play. The Redskins and the Dolphins got hot and won their divisions, then slogged through three rounds of postseason play to reach the big game.

The Redskins had not been to the playoffs since the mid-1970s. Coach Joe Gibbs decided that the best way to get back there was to play simple, straightforward football. He assembled a massive front line, lured 240-pound (109-kg) fullback John Riggins out of retirement, gave aging Joe Theisman a couple of sure-handed receivers, and helped rejuvenate kicker Mark Moseley. By 1982, all the pieces were in place—including a bend-but-don't-break defense that starred lineman Dexter Manley and defensive backs Vernon Dean and Tony Peters.

The Dolphins had hoped to have first-round draft choice David Overstreet in their backfield, but he surprised them and signed with the Canadian Football League. Instead, Don Shula took the players he had in camp and molded them into a dependable unit. Emerging from the pack was running back Andra Franklin and guard Ed Newman, who both enjoyed career years. Second-year quarterback David Woodley progressed as well as expected, with Don

Strock providing quality relief from the bench. The defensive unit was nicknamed the "Killer Bees" because more than half of the starters had last names beginning with the letter *B*. The best of the Bees was Bob Baumhower, who distinguished himself as one of the great nose tackles in history.

The only clear advantage either team had in this contest was in the running department. Riggins gave the Redskins a weapon that the Dolphins had no effective way of countering. All the other matchups were fairly even. Shula's strategy was a smart one: Score quickly and make Theisman play catch-up. This would force the quarterback to throw, thus making Riggins less of a factor.

Shula looked like a genius on Miami's second possession. Woodley dropped back from his own 24-yard line and rifled the ball to receiver Jimmy Cefalo just across midfield. Cefalo outran Peters to the end zone

As the Dolphins discovered in Super Bowl XVII, it took more than one tackler to stop John Riggins.

IN THE NICK OF TEAM

Few Super Bowl champs enjoyed themselves as much as the Redskins. After touchdowns, the "Fun Bunch" gathered in the end zone for a special high-five celebration.

The Washington Redskins led the NFL in only a couple of statistical categories in 1982. No team in the league, however, had more nicknames. Washington's offensive linemen—Joe Jacoby, Russ Grimm, Jeff Bostic, Fred Dean, and George Starke—nicknamed themselves the "Hogs" because they liked to get down and dirty. The team's trio of pint-sized receivers—Charlie Brown, Alvin Garrett, and Virgil Seay—were known as the "Smurfs." The players (pictured at left) who performed the carefully choreographed end zone celebrations for the Redskins were called the "Fun Bunch."

So what did the Redskins call stern and serious Joe Gibbs? "Coach." They knew where to draw the line!

to give the Dolphins a 7-0 lead. Washington got on the board early in the second quarter after Manley hammered Woodley and Dave Butz jumped on the loose ball. Moseley, who was 20-for-21 in field goals during the season, split the uprights four plays later to make it a 7-3 game.

Uwe von Schamann made a 20-yard field goal for the Dolphins, but Theisman countered with an 80-yard drive that ended with a short pass to Alvin Garrett in the end zone. With the score 10-10, Miami re-

turn specialist Fulton Walker—who already had one spectacular run in the game—took Moseley's kickoff, found a seam, and went all the way for a 98-yard score. The Redskins mounted a charge in the final minutes but ran out of time deep in Miami territory.

The Miami players went into the locker room on a high. Surprisingly, so did the Redskins. Although trailing 17-10, they sensed that they had the Dolphins right where they wanted them.

Washington trimmed Miami's lead to 17-13 during a hard-fought third quarter. The Dolphins, who were starting to tire, failed to score during the period. Their best chance came when Kim Bokamper batted a Theisman pass straight up in the air. Everyone froze as the big defensive end waited for the ball to come down—everyone, that is, except Theisman. Realizing that he was the only person standing between Bokamper and the end zone, he jumped up and punched the ball to the ground before it was intercepted. It turned out to be a game-saving play.

Early in the fourth quarter, Theisman and Riggins attempted a flea-flicker, but the quarterback's pass to Charlie Brown was intercepted by Lyle Blackwood near the goal line. The Washington defense kept Woodley from breaking out, and Tom Orosz's punt barely crossed midfield. This appeared to be the chance that the Redskins had been waiting for. Three running plays gained 9 yards and set up a fourth-and-1 on the Dolphins' 43-yard line. Coach Gibbs opted to go for the first down. He was confident that his defense could stop the Dolphins if the decision backfired.

The Redskins called their best play, a run through the left side of the line. Before the snap, tight end Clint Didier went in motion to the right, then abruptly turned back left. Cornerback Don McNeal, following him on defense, slipped when he tried to reverse field. Riggins took the handoff and headed for the hole. He saw immediately that the Dolphins had plugged it up, so he bounced outside, hoping that he could turn the corner before the cornerback tackled him. The cornerback was McNeal, who still was trying to get back to his original spot. Riggins found no one at home and just kept running. A short-yardage call became a 43-yard touchdown!

Leading 20-17, the Redskins halted Miami's next drive and began to work time off the clock. Again and again, Riggins pounded the ball into the line, picking up precious first downs behind his big blockers. At the Dolphins' 9-yard line, Theisman rolled out and hit Brown with a touchdown pass to make the final score 27-17.

> **Redskins 27**
> **Dolphins 17**
>   Best Player: John Riggins

Super Bowl XVIII
January 22, 1984
(1983 Season)
Washington Redskins (NFC)
vs. Los Angeles Raiders (AFC)

The Washington Redskins returned to the Super Bowl to defend their championship against the Los Angeles Raiders. Both teams were well coached and stocked with veterans, and each brought more than a little attitude into the game. The Redskins were the NFL's bully—they went chin-to-chin with opponents and just overwhelmed them. The Raiders were the league's back-alley brawlers—tough, sneaky, and not above kicking or clawing if that's what it took to get the job done.

The Redskins went into the 1983 season with something to prove. Their Super Bowl title was considered tarnished because of the previous year's strike. In a full season, many contended, Washington might not even have won its division. The Redskins erased any doubt that they were the NFC's top team by finishing with a 14-2 record and rolling up big scores against virtually every opponent. The cast of characters was the same as in 1982, but injuries, holdouts, and age were taking their toll on the defense. The offense made up the difference, with John Riggins running for 24 touchdowns and Joe Theisman throwing for 29.

The Raiders, in their second year in Los Angeles, had improved since their last Super Bowl appearance. Defensive end Howie Long, just 23 years old, had turned into a superstar. Marcus Allen, in his second year as a pro, ran for 1,014 yards and caught 68 passes. Todd Christensen provided an unexpected bonus with 92 catches and 12 touchdowns. The Raider offensive line and linebacking crew were still solid, while the defensive secondary got a boost from the acquisition of All-Pro Mike Haynes. The final piece of the puzzle was veteran leader Jim Plunkett, who again had come off the bench to become the starting quarterback. Simply put, the Raiders were loaded.

Most everyone agreed that this game would come down to how well the Washington defense handled the Los Angeles offense. The Redskins had given up a lot of points, including five touchdowns, to the Raiders in an October meeting that Washington had won 37-35. The Redskins had a great offense, too, but Tom Flores was confident that his defense could contain Theisman and Riggins. For Joe Gibbs, the key to winning was to control the game and not to let the emotional Raiders gain the momentum.

Things broke the Raiders' way 5 minutes into the first quarter. Washington punter Jeff Hayes had his kick blocked by Los Angeles special-teams captain Derrick Jensen, who then tracked down the loose ball in the end zone for seven points. The Redskins wasted a chance to get on the board when Mark Moseley missed a 44-yard field goal.

In the second quarter, Plunkett spotted Cliff Branch sprinting through a Washington double-team and hit him for a 50-yard gain. They connected again in the end zone to put Los Angeles up 14-0. The Redskins knew they had to score before the half, or they would be forced to throw in the third and fourth quarters. Theisman put together a 13-play drive but had to settle for a field goal when the Raider defense stiffened deep in its own territory.

The Redskins got the ball back on their own 12-yard line right before halftime, and everyone assumed they would just run out the clock. Hoping to catch the Raiders napping, Gibbs called a short screen pass. The Raiders, sensing that something was up, inserted Jack Squirek into the game for starter Matt Millen. Squirek stood 6-foot-4 (1.93 m) with long arms, and he was superb at defending short passes. Theisman took the snap and dropped back. His blockers allowed the pass rushers through, creating the screen for which the play is named. Waiting for the ball on the other side was running back Joe Washington. As Theisman released the ball, Squirek was already running toward Washington. He plucked the ball out of the air and ran into the end zone for a touchdown with just 7 seconds left.

In the locker room, Gibbs reminded his players that they had scored 17 points in the final 6 minutes the last time the two teams played. Yes, they were down, but they were hardly out. In the Raider locker room, the players were wide-eyed and excited. They could smell a wipeout. This was exactly what Washington hoped to avoid.

CHARLIE ON THE SPOT

When Charlie Sumner played for the Bears and the Vikings in the 1950s and 1960s, not much escaped his attention. A defensive back out of William and Mary, he won a starting spot as a rookie and became an instant target for the league's quarterbacks. Learning on the job, he more than held his own; seven times he intercepted enemy passes. After spending two years in the military, Sumner rejoined the Bears and was tested again. This time he picked off six passes. Finally, the NFL wised up and stopped throwing his way. Sumner obviously knew something that they did not.

Fast-forward 25 years, to the end of the second quarter in Super Bowl XVIII.

Charlie Sumner, the linebacker coach of the Los Angeles Raiders, saw something in the Redskins' huddle that made him think a screen pass was coming. Instantly, he sent backup linebacker Jack

As a player, Charlie Sumner made his mark as a ball-hawking defensive back with the Bears and the Vikings. As a linebacker coach, his instincts turned the tide in Super Bowl XVIII.

Squirek into the game for starter Matt Millen. Sumner's thinking was simple: With more height and a broader wingspan, Squirek might get to a ball that Millen would miss.

Sumner's hunch was correct. Joe Theisman attempted the screen pass that the Raiders were expecting, and Squirek picked it out of the air and ran for a touchdown. The Redskins never recovered from this play.

Washington got back in the game with a long touchdown drive to open the second half. The Raiders blocked Moseley's extra point, keeping the score at 21-9. Plunkett came right back with a 70-yard drive, which was kept alive when rookie Darrell Green was penalized for pass interference. Allen finished off the march with a 5-yard scamper up the middle to give Los Angeles a 28-9 lead.

Washington had trouble moving the ball for the rest of the quarter, but they caught a break when Branch fumbled on his own 35-yard line. After advancing 9 yards in three plays, Theisman faced a crucial fourth

down. The Redskins were too far behind to go for a field goal; they needed a first down and then a touchdown. Everyone in Tampa Stadium knew who was getting the ball, including linebacker Rod Martin. Martin, the defensive hero of Super Bowl XV, shed a block and met Riggins head on to stop him for no gain. The play ripped the heart out of the Redskins. On the very next play, Plunkett handed off to Allen, who sprinted 74 yards for a touchdown.

The dejected Redskins could muster little offense in the fourth quarter. The Raiders sacked Theisman three times and intercepted him once. With just over 2 minutes left, Los Angeles added a field goal to put the final nail in Washington's coffin. With their unique mix of power and passion, the Raiders had laid the Redskins to rest.

> **Raiders 38**
> **Redskins 9**
> **Best Player: Marcus Allen**

Marcus Allen ran wild on the Redskins, including a record-setting 74-yard touchdown romp.

Super Bowl XIX
January 20, 1985
(1984 Season)
San Francisco 49ers (NFC)
vs. Miami Dolphins (AFC)

After two strange and disappointing seasons, the San Francisco 49ers returned to the Super Bowl with a monster team. Their opponents, the Miami Dolphins, rode the amazing arm of 22-year-old Dan Marino to the AFC championship. For the first time since 1979, the two best quarterbacks of their era were meeting in the Super Bowl.

The 49ers had come close to making this their fourth trip to the big game. The

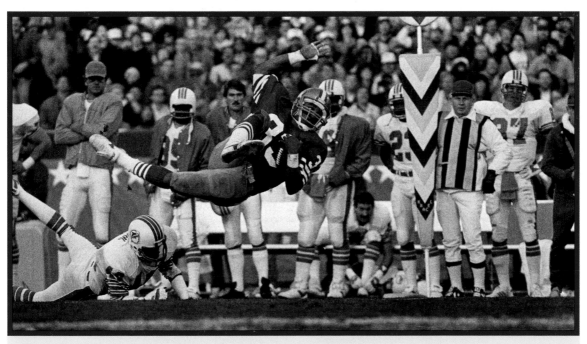

Versatile Roger Craig (#33) was the key to San Francisco's "West Coast" offense. He led the 49ers in carries and receptions in Super Bowl XIX.

1982 strike hit them hard, however, and their 1983 Super Bowl run was derailed in the NFC Championship when two questionable late-game penalties gave the Redskins a three-point win. In 1984, Coach Bill Walsh further refined his "West Coast" offense with the addition of Roger Craig, a magnificent fullback who could grind out tough yards and catch the ball like a receiver. Craig and Wendell Tyler combined for nearly 3,000 running and receiving yards, which helped Joe Montana to finish the year as the NFC's top-ranked quarterback.

The Dolphins were returning to the Super Bowl with the same solid defense but a completely retooled offense. Marino, who had grabbed the starter's job a year earlier as a rookie, had a season that might never be duplicated. His quick release and strong, accurate arm had caught opponents com-

pletely by surprise—and for 16 games he did pretty much as he pleased. Working with a pair of dynamic young receivers—Mark Duper and Mark Clayton—Marino threw for 5,084 yards and 48 touchdowns. The former University of Pittsburgh quarterback was literally unstoppable. In Miami's only two losses, the team still scored 62 points! The Miami running game was good, too. Four backs—Woody Bennett, Tony Nathan, Joe Carter, and ex-Bengal Pete Johnson—gave Don Shula a lot of options when he chose to run the ball.

Although football fans loved the glamorous Dolphins, San Francisco was given the edge in what promised to be the highest-scoring Super Bowl yet. The 49ers had the experience, as well as the league's best pass defense. Both cornerbacks and both safeties were voted to the All-Pro team. Marino had never faced a defense quite this good.

A TALE OF TWO QUARTERBACKS

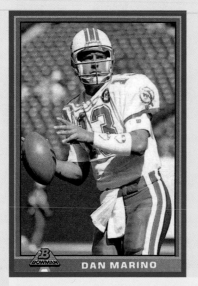 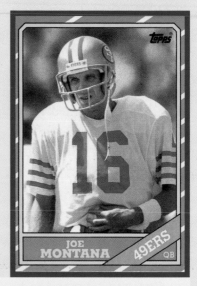

The Super Bowl matchup between Dan Marino and Joe Montana fueled tremendous interest in the two superstars among memorabilia collectors.

No one has ever had the kind of season Dan Marino did in 1984. In his second NFL campaign, he threw for 5,084 yards and 48 touchdowns. Every reporter in the week leading up to Super Bowl XIX followed his every move and hung on his every word.

This surprised and angered a lot of the 49ers. Forget the statistics—they felt they had the game's best quarterback. The team had just won a record 15 games and shut out the Bears in the NFC championship 23-0. What else, they wondered, did Joe Montana have to do to get a little respect?

At first, Montana did not care. He had been through the media madness of a Super Bowl once before, and he welcomed the peace and quiet. As game day approached, however, his teammates noticed that the modest, quiet Montana was getting a little annoyed. By game time, he was taking it personally. Not that "Super Joe" ever needed extra motivation to win a Super Bowl, but this time he wanted it badly.

Once the game began, the difference between the two quarterbacks emerged. Marino had the rifle arm, but Montana was the sniper. Marino's statistics were okay—he threw for over 300 yards and a touchdown—but his three interceptions destroyed Miami. Montana completed 69 percent of his passes for 331 yards, 3 touchdowns, and no interceptions. What really killed the Dolphins, however, were plays that did not show up in Montana's stats. On several key downs, with Miami guessing pass, Montana crossed them up with running plays that went for big gains.

In the first quarter, both quarterbacks played superbly. Marino guided the Dolphins into scoring position on their first possession. Uwe von Schamann connected on a 33-yard field goal to make the score 3-0. Not to be outdone, Montana immediately directed the 49ers to a touchdown, lofting a 33-yard scoring strike to reserve running back Carl Monroe. Marino warmed to the challenge. When Miami got the ball back, he capped an impressive drive with a 2-yard touchdown pass to tight end Dan Johnson. After a quarter, the Dolphins led 10-7.

In the second period, Montana began probing Miami's defense for soft spots while Coach Walsh shuffled players in and out of the lineup, hoping to confuse the Dolphins and to exploit uneven matchups. As the quarter unfolded, San Francisco realized that it had a major advantage on the left side of the line. Tackle Bubba Paris was manhandling defensive end Kim Bokamper, whom he outweighed by about 50 pounds (23 kg). Whenever the 49ers needed a few yards, Montana sent one of his runners into this part of the line.

Helped by several poor punts by Miami's Reggie Roby, the 49ers scored on three straight possessions. Montana threw to running back Roger Craig for an 8-yard touchdown to make the score 14-10. Later Montana scored on a short run. Finally, Craig barreled into the end zone from 2 yards out to put San Francisco up 28-10. Marino salvaged the half with a drive that resulted in another field goal. The Dolphins added three more points after 49er Guy McIntyre fumbled the squib kickoff, and Miami recovered with enough time for Von Schamann to boot his third three-pointer of the game.

Lucky to be down by just 12 points, the Dolphins knew they would have to rely heavily on their passing game in the second half. Although this was Miami's strength, it also played right into San Francisco's game plan.

The Dolphins looked good on their first drive of the second half, but a third-down sack by defensive end Dwaine Board took them out of field-goal range. The 49ers moved the ball swiftly down the field for a field goal of their own to make the score 31-16. Two more sacks of Marino on Miami's next drive set the tone for the rest of the half. The Dolphins never threatened again.

San Francisco scored its final touchdown on terrific pass plays to Tyler, Russ Francis, and Craig. With the score 38-16 and an entire quarter left to play, the 49ers ran out the clock on offense and bottled up Marino on defense. Although the game featured six touchdowns, it was not the shootout everyone had hoped for. The 49ers were too well coached to get into that kind of game.

49ers 38
Dolphins 16
Best Player: Joe Montana

Super Bowl XX
January 26, 1986
(1985 Season)
Chicago Bears (NFC) vs.
New England Patriots (AFC)

Defense wins Super Bowls. Year in, year out, the NFL champion is the team that plays the toughest "D" when it has to. The 1985 Chicago Bears were the toughest defensive unit most people had ever seen.

Their opponents were the New England Patriots, a Wild Card team that suddenly became an overachiever after years of squandering its talent. Everyone was predicting a Super Bowl slaughter.

New England had just enough weapons to win in a year when no AFC team stood out as a top contender. Quarterbacks Tony Eason and Steve Grogan directed an offense that featured solid runners—Craig James and Tony Collins—and cat-quick receivers—Stanley Morgan and Irving Fryar. The key to the Pats' offense was its front line, which boasted the best left side in football, with All-Pros Brian Holloway and John Hannah. The New England defense was led by linebacker Andre Tippett and defensive backs Ray Clayborn and Fred Marion.

The Chicago defense was simply awesome. There was a talented player at every position, and most were in the prime years of their careers. The front line was anchored by Richard Dent, Dan Hampton, and 350-pound (160-kg) rookie William "The Refrigerator" Perry. The linebacking corps was headed by superstar Mike Singletary. The secondary, which picked off 23 passes, starred safeties Gary Fencik and Dave Duerson. The Bears had a good offense, too. Quarterback Jim McMahon was the team's courageous field leader, and veteran back Walter Payton was its best player. Chicago scored the most points in the NFC, gave up the fewest, and ended its dominant season with shutouts over the Giants and the 49ers in the playoffs.

Cocky and confident, the Bears were all swagger when they took the field for their opening series. Moments later, Chicago fans watched in horror as Payton fumbled and the Patriots took over on the 19-yard line. The Bears held, and Tony Franklin kicked a field goal to give New England an unexpected 3-0 lead.

On Chicago's next possession, McMahon completed a long pass to former Olympic sprinter Willie Gault, and this set up a game-tying field goal by Kevin Butler. Butler scored again after Dent's sack of Eason forced a turnover deep in New England territory. A second Patriot fumble, by James, gave Chicago another scoring chance. This time the Bears reached the end zone for a 13-3 lead.

Eason seemed confused and disoriented. Coach Raymond Berry replaced him with Grogan, but the veteran could not solve the Chicago defense either. Meanwhile, McMahon poured it on. He led the Bears on a 59-yard drive and carried the ball over the goal line himself to make it 20-3. Another Butler field goal before halftime gave the Bears a 23-3 advantage.

The Patriots had no answers. They had allowed the Bears to amass 236 yards in the first two periods, while their yardage stood at an embarrassing -13. In the Chicago locker room, the players decided they would go for the biggest Super Bowl wipeout ever.

On their first possession of the third quarter, the Bears struck again on another long pass from McMahon to Gault. With the ball on the 2-yard line, McMahon did the honors himself, sneaking into the end zone to make the score 30-3. The Bears added another seven points when cornerback Reggie Phillips intercepted Grogan on the 28-yard line and returned it for a touchdown.

Incredibly, the worst was yet to come for the poor Patriots. After fumbling again in their own territory, they watched as coach Mike Ditka sent Perry into the game as a

Steve McMichael and William Perry carry coach Mike Ditka off the field after wiping out the Patriots in Super Bowl XX. By this time many viewers had already turned off their TVs.

running back. The Refrigerator lined up behind McMahon in a three-point stance, flab pouring out of his too-tight uniform, took the handoff, and bowled over a couple of New England tacklers for the game's final touchdown.

With the outcome decided, the Patriots managed to score a fourth-quarter touchdown when Grogan hit Morgan with a 28-yard pass. The Bears defense took this personally, and on New England's next possession, Grogan found himself flattened under the Chicago pass rush in his own end zone for a safety.

Although the Bears' dominant performance had been interesting to watch, the game itself offered little in the way of excitement for fans. Not since the Steelers' comeback against the Rams six years earlier had the Super Bowl had much suspense. By this time it had become the ultimate sport-

ing event in North America—more people watched the Super Bowl than any other contest. As a game, however, the Super Bowl was in danger of losing some of its luster.

> **Bears 46**
> **Patriots 10**
> Best Player: Richard Dent

Super Bowl XXI
January 25, 1987
(1986 Season)
New York Giants (NFC)
vs. Denver Broncos (AFC)

The 1986 season looked like it would belong to the Bears again. Their defense was even better than it was in 1985, and despite a season-ending injury to Jim McMahon,

LIGHTS! CAMERA! ACTION!

The "Fridge" celebrates a rushing touchdown by spiking the football. The Bears were both colorful and cocky.

Football teams don't get points for personality, but if any team deserved to, it was the Chicago Bears. What a collection of characters! At the top of the list were fiery Coach Mike Ditka and rebellious quarterback Jim McMahon. They could be best friends one day and at each other's throats the next. William "Refrigerator" Perry, the overweight lineman with the gap-toothed smile, was irresistibly charming. Defensive end Dan "The Animal" Hampton, with his gigantic arms and shoulder-length hair, was scarier out of his uniform than in it.

Gary Fencik, a graduate of Yale, had the air of a future politician, while soft-spoken Walter "Sweetness" Payton was the nicest guy who ever left a cleat mark in your chest. The team's defensive leader, Mike "Samurai" Singletary, was an accomplished martial artist. Kicker Kevin Butler was into butting heads with teammates whenever he made a field goal. And the list goes on and on.

If you're thinking these guys should have been in a video, you're right. And they were! Prior to the game, the team got together in a studio and performed *The Super Bowl Shuffle*. It was the nation's top video for several weeks, and it began a trend that caused dozens of teams to make their own videos. No one's, however, was as good as the Bears'.

the offense was good enough to win 14 games. All that remained was to figure out which AFC team they would humiliate in the Super Bowl after taking care of the 49ers in the NFC title game. The playoffs turned that picture upside-down, however. The Wild Card Redskins stunned Chicago 27-13, and the New York Giants throttled San Francisco 49-3. When the Giants shut out Washington 17-0, they earned the right to play John Elway and the Denver Broncos for the championship of pro football.

When the season started, the Giants looked like a club on the verge of something special, but the timing was terrible. The Bears and the 49ers, at the peak of their powers, presented daunting obstacles to the New Yorkers. In a midseason game against San Francisco, the Giants fell behind 17-0 in a humiliating first half. As Giants fans watched Joe Montana pick their defense apart, they sensed that they were witnessing a preview of what would happen in the playoffs. Then, in the second half, something unexpected occurred. Quarterback Phil Simms managed to solve the 49er defense, and the Giants defense shut Montana down. New York won 21-17 and rolled through the rest of its schedule confident that it could beat anyone.

The Giants were a team that won by crushing opponents with defense. Their star was Lawrence Taylor, or "LT," a linebacker who seemed to play the game at a different

New York fans who criticized the Giants for drafting unknown Phil Simms changed their tune after his near-perfect performance against the Denver Broncos in Super Bowl XXI.

speed than everyone else. Working off the havoc that LT created, fellow linebackers Harry Carson, Carl Banks, and Gary Reasons were free to gamble on the kind of game-turning plays that enabled the Giants to finish with a surprising 14-2 record. The offense, led by Simms and running back Joe Morris, was conservative and precise. Coach Bill Parcells let his quarterback know he would not have it any other way.

The Broncos were anything but conservative. When Elway had the ball in his hands, he could beat you in a dozen different ways. He could throw long or short, hard or soft—and he could run as well as most fullbacks. Elway took more chances (and made more mistakes) than coach Dan Reeves would have liked, but he usually made up for his errors with thrilling comebacks. (Denver's AFC opponents had a term for losing to the Broncos in the final minutes. They called it "getting Elway-ed.") Because the team played a lot of close games, it relied heavily on its defense. Featured here were linebacker Tom Jackson and cornerback Louis Wright (both holdovers from Denver's 1978 Super Bowl squad), as well as Karl Mecklenberg, Dennis Smith, and Rulon Jones.

The Giants had defeated the Broncos 19-16 a couple of months earlier. In that game, Parcells had learned that the best way to contain Elway was to cover his receivers man-to-man and to make him stay in the pocket and complete tough throws. Meanwhile, the Broncos had learned that the Giants could be beaten by keeping constant pressure on Simms. In Super Bowl XXI's opening moments, Elway made one of those tough throws to receiver Mark Jackson, who picked up 24 yards. He could do no more, however, and the Broncos had to

settle for a long field goal by Rich Karlis. The Denver defense was less successful against Simms, who took his time and completed six straight passes on New York's first drive. The final throw fell into the arms of tight end Zeke Mowatt, whose touchdown gave the Giants a 7-3 lead.

Elway wasted no time regaining the momentum. With the aid of a double penalty on Carson, Denver moved the ball down to the 4-yard line. Elway fooled everyone by taking the snap and pretending he was going to drop back and pass. At just the right moment he shifted direction and scored right up the middle on a "quarterback draw." Late in the first quarter, Elway entered the "red zone" again. This time the Giants made a magnificent goal-line stand, and Karlis botched a 23-yard field-goal attempt.

The game settled into a defensive battle in the second quarter. Neither team was able to mount much of an attack. The only score came when Elway was sacked in his own end zone. The Broncos made one last push into New York territory, but Karlis missed another field goal. At halftime, Denver held a slim 10-9 lead.

In the locker room, Parcells told his players that they had been lucky. In the second half they would have to be good. No one took this message to heart more than Simms, who knew that he needed to put more points on the board. The Broncos had few worries. Their offense was moving well, and they would have had 16 points were it not for two missed kicks. Outside of New York's opening drive, the Broncos had not allowed the Giants to get close to another score. Simms would have to play perfect football to do any damage in the second half.

After their first series of the second half

MAN WITH A PLAN

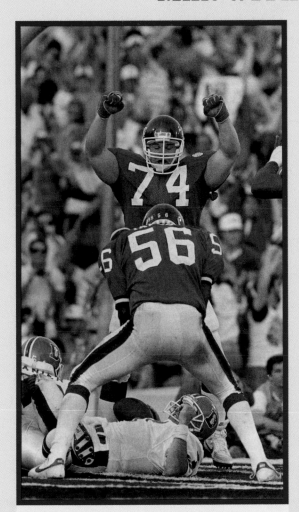

Defensive superstar Lawrence Taylor (#56) was a relentless pursuer who revolutionized the way his position was played. He was the centerpiece of New York's legendary linebacking corps.

When defensive coordinator Bill Parcells took over as head coach for the long-suffering Giants in 1983, he had a plan: Build a defense around great linebackers, and then build an offense around your defense. Parcells began with a solid foundation. Lawrence Taylor, in his third season, was just coming into his own. Harry Carson was in his prime. And veterans Brian Kelley and Brad Van Pelt were still good enough to teach the young guys a thing or two.

In 1984, Parcells cut loose Van Pelt and Kelley and replaced them with rookies Carl Banks and Gary Reasons. The Giants had the best defense in their division; their win total soared from three to nine; and the team grabbed a Wild Card spot in the playoffs. Two years later, Taylor, Carson, Banks, and Reasons—along with subs Andy Headen, Byron Hunt, and Pepper Johnson—formed the greatest linebacking corps since the glory days of the Pittsburgh Steelers. The Giants outscored their opponents 371 to 236 and went 14-2. Throughout the season, and particularly in the postseason, the linebackers made one game-winning play after another.

The secret of Parcells's success was clearest in the team's dramatic goal-line stand against the Broncos in Super Bowl XXI. On first down, Taylor hounded John Elway until he stopped him for a 1-yard loss. On second down, Carson stuffed Gerald Willhite on a trap play up the middle. On third down, Banks tackled Sammy Winder for a 4-yard loss on a sweep to the left. Denver learned the hard way that you don't mess with Parcells's boys.

stalled at midfield, the Giants decided to shake things up. Parcells called for a fake punt. Reserve quarterback Jeff Rutledge grabbed the snap and bulled forward 2 yards to keep the drive alive. Simms came back on and took the team all the way to the end zone, with a final play to tight end Mark Bavaro.

At this point, Simms sensed that he had the Denver defense right where he wanted it. In the first half, he had run nine pass plays on first down. This had confused the Broncos, who kept expecting Simms to hand off to Morris. Because Denver used different players on obvious passing downs, the coaching staff was not sure which player to send out on the field. For the rest of the game, Simms could scan the defense, pick out a Bronco who was not a strong pass defender, and then isolate him by calling a play for the receiver he was supposed to cover.

Simms took the Giants into Denver territory again, and Raul Allegre booted a short field goal to make the score 19-10. New York mounted yet another scoring drive in the third quarter. Denver expected Simms to pass on first down, but he made handoffs to Morris twice for hefty first-down gains. The Broncos were faked out of their pants on one play, when Morris got the ball and then whipped around and pitched back to Simms, who delivered a long pass to receiver Phil McConkey. Morris took the ball over from 1 yard out to give New York a 26-10 lead.

Denver cut into that margin with a fourth-quarter field goal by Karlis, but it was too late. Simms orchestrated yet another touchdown drive, this time completing a pass to McConkey that bounced off of Bavaro in the end zone. The Giants could do no wrong. They traded touchdowns with the Broncos right before the 2-minute warning, and the final score was 39-20.

The New York defense had challenged Elway to beat them. He could not, despite passing for more than 300 yards. Simms knew he had to be almost perfect to execute his plan. He was. The golden-haired quarterback played his best in the biggest game of his life, completing 22 of 25 passes for 268 yards.

> **Giants 39**
> **Broncos 20**
> **Best Player: Phil Simms**

Super Bowl XXII
January 31, 1988
(1987 Season)
Washington Redskins (NFC)
vs. Denver Broncos (AFC)

You never know how things are going to work out in the NFL. When Dan Marino left the field after Super Bowl XIX, he assumed that he would return one day. He never made it to another Super Bowl. The AFC's other young gun, John Elway, took his team back to the big game a year later, despite having his offense overhauled at midseason. On the other side of the ball were the Washington Redskins, playing in the Super Bowl for the third time in the 1980s. They began the year with a young passer who seemed destined for greatness (Jay Schroeder), then won the NFC championship with a quarterback they pulled off the pro-football scrap heap (Doug Williams).

Williams, the first African-American quarterback to hold down a long-term starting job in the NFL, had guided the Tampa Bay Buccaneers from the bottom of the standings to the NFC championship game during the

Redskins fans show support for their beloved "hogs" prior to Washington's wipeout of the Denver Broncos.

late 1970s. When the Redskins called, however, he was back at the bottom of the pile, out of work and seemingly out of chances. Signed as a backup to Schroeder, he was promoted by coach Joe Gibbs when the quality of Schroeder's performance became unpredictable from week to week. The 32-year-old Williams did little more than hand off in playoff wins against the Bears and Vikings, and he was not expected to do much else during the Super Bowl.

The rest of the Redskins did not exactly strike fear into the hearts of Denver fans. The defense made big plays but also gave them up. Washington was especially vulnerable to the pass, which was Elway's specialty. The team's lone offensive star was receiver Gary Clark. The Hogs were still going strong, but the backs they blocked for were not. George Rogers was injured; Kelvin Bryant was more of a receiver than a

runner; and Keith Vital, Lionel Griffin, and Timmy Smith lacked size and experience.

The Broncos, meanwhile, seemed to be coming into their own. Between injuries and retirements, Denver had to make a number of adjustments during the regular season. In the ninth game, Dan Reeves switched to a shotgun offense, in which the quarterback receives the snap several yards behind the center. This gave Elway a great view of the field, and he finished the season strong. In this pass-oriented offense, receivers Vinnie Johnson, Mark Jackson, and Ricky Nattiel prospered. The change also helped the team's running game. The only major hurdle for the Broncos was the Cleveland Browns, who put up a great fight in the AFC championship game for the second year in a row.

As expected, the Broncos took control of Super Bowl XXII right away. Just 2 minutes into the game, Elway and Nattiel hooked up for a beautiful 56-yard touchdown. Later in the first quarter, Elway caught a ball from running back Steve Sewell on a trick play that caught the Redskins by surprise. The play set up a field goal by Rich Karlis, who gave the Broncos a 10-0 lead.

Meanwhile, Washington struggled on offense. When Williams twisted his knee and hobbled to the sideline, it looked like the beginning of a long day for Coach Gibbs. While on the sideline, Williams was able to regain his focus. and he reentered the field more confident about Washington's game plan.

On the first play of the second quarter, with the ball at his own 20-yard line, Williams called for a short hitch pass to Ricky Sanders. When Sanders was bumped off his pattern, he veered down the field and into the open. Seeing this develop, Williams

A MOMENT OF PERFECTION

SUPER BOWL MOMENTS

Doug Williams
340-YARD PASSING PERFORMANCE

This trading card depicts a cool, confident Doug Williams in the midst of his record-smashing performance. Williams threw for four touchdowns in the second quarter.

A lifetime of expectations, achievement, and despair went into the making of Doug Williams's unforgettable second quarter in Super Bowl XXII. Born in Louisiana, Williams lived with nine other family members in a five-room house without indoor plumbing. His first football was a plastic jug (he could not afford a real ball), and his first love was baseball. A sidearm pitcher, Williams threw three no-hitters at Chaneyville High but did not go out for the football team until he was 17.

A year later, the rifle-armed teenager was offered a scholarship to Grambling State University, where he starred for legendary Coach Eddie Robinson and tossed a record 93 touchdowns. In 1978, Williams became the first African-American quarterback ever selected in the first round of the NFL draft. As a rookie with the Tampa Bay Buccaneers, he started ten games—including one with his shattered jaw wired shut—and quickly reversed the fortunes of football's worst team. The Bucs had gone 2-26 in their first two NFL seasons. In Williams's second season, he guided them all the way to the NFC championship game.

Williams racked up nearly 10,000 passing yards over the next three seasons, and he got the Bucs into the playoffs twice. When the United States Football League was formed in the early 1980s, he signed a five-year deal with the Oklahoma Out-laws. He was riding high.

Then his world came crashing down. In the spring of 1983, his wife, Janice, died of a brain tumor. Williams, left to raise his daughter alone, moved back to Louisiana to be with his family. Rather than building his dream home in a fancy suburb, he constructed it a stone's throw from the ramshackle house where he grew up. He coached a girl's softball team. He held family barbecues for hundreds of relatives. Williams began to see that family was more important than football, and he discovered new ways to fit football into his life.

These revelations buoyed Williams when the USFL folded. He was out of a job, and he had little chance of getting any of the money owed to him. Now, however, it didn't matter as much. If the NFL wanted him back, he was ready. If not, he was ready for that, too.

Williams waited for the phone to ring. And waited. And waited. Finally the call came. It was his old offensive coordinator with the Buccaneers, Joe Gibbs, now one of the most highly respected head coaches in the NFL. Gibbs asked Williams if he would be willing to join the Washington Redskins—not as a starter, but as a backup. Had anyone else called, the answer might have been no.

Williams got into one game in 1986 and attempted just one pass. The starter, Jay Schroeder, was young and strong and having a brilliant season. In 1987, Williams returned for a second year as a Washington benchwarmer. This time Schroeder was not so brilliant. Twice in the early part of the season, Gibbs sent Williams in to relieve Schroeder, and twice the veteran pulled off dramatic comebacks. By the end of the year, Williams had won the starting job.

Talent and experience enabled Williams to make key plays in close playoff wins over the Bears and Vikings, and suddenly the Redskins were in the Super Bowl. In the days leading up to the big game, Williams was the center of attention. Hundreds of reporters were looking for interesting story angles. As the first African-American quarterback to start a Super Bowl, Williams was a natural. He patiently answered question after question—some very personal and some very stupid. One reporter actually asked him how long he had been a black quarterback.

Williams was highly focused (and no doubt relieved) by the time Super Bowl XXII started. And of course, in the second quarter, every play went just right. For a man whose life and career had turned out far from perfect, it was a moment of absolute perfection.

threw a perfect strike to Sanders. The swift wideout tucked the ball away and ran all the way to the end zone for an 80-yard touchdown. The game was back under control, with the Redskins trailing only 10-7.

On Washington's next possession, Williams called the same play for Clark as he had for Sanders. When Clark got jostled out of his route, he too went long. Once again, Williams caught the adjustment and delivered a perfect pass—this one for a 27-yard touchdown to give the Redskins a 14-10 lead. Denver clawed its way back into Washington territory but came up short when Karlis missed a field-goal attempt from 43 yards away. The Redskins took over, and Williams called a running play for Smith, the rookie running back. The 22-year-old out of Texas Tech squeezed through an opening in the line and then broke outside. This time, the receivers were doing the jostling. They threw the blocks that enabled Smith to race 58 yards for the third touchdown of the period.

After Denver failed to advance on its next possession, Williams took over again. He faked a handoff up the middle to freeze the safety, whose job was to prevent another big run. By the time he realized Williams intended to pass, however, Sanders had gotten behind him and was in the clear. Again, Williams hit his man, this time for a 50-yard touchdown. It was now 28-10, and the end of the quarter was still several minutes away. In a panic to come back, Elway threw a devastating interception. Back on the field came the Washington offensive unit. Williams sent Sanders and tight end Clint Didier to the same spot and waited in the pocket to see which receiver would not be covered. It was Didier, and he hit him with a 9-yard spiral for the

Redskins' fifth touchdown of the period—a Super Bowl record.

The second half featured a lot less scoring. The Redskins, with almost no chance of losing, concentrated on running down the clock. They fed Smith the ball again and again, and he played the game of his life with 204 yards—78 more than he had amassed all season! Poor Elway, trying to conserve time and to move his team quickly, dropped back to pass on more than half the remaining plays. The Washington defense blitzed him mercilessly, and he was unable to mount even one scoring drive. The game ended 42-10.

To this day, no one can explain what happened during the second quarter of Super Bowl XXII. It stands as the most amazing 15 minutes of football ever played in a championship game.

Redskins 42
Broncos 10
  Best Player: Doug Williams

Super Bowl XXIII
January 22, 1989
(1988 Season)
San Francisco 49ers (NFC)
vs. Cincinnati Bengals (AFC)

The 1988 Cincinnati Bengals were among the slickest teams ever to take a football field. They had an MVP quarterback, a big-game runner, solid receivers, an excellent defense, and terrific special teams. They would need it all to contend with the San Francisco 49ers, who were on a spectacular roll.

Building on the runaway success of his teams in the early 1980s, Bill Walsh assembled a squad that was full of All-Pros and future Hall of Famers. The offense was still run by Joe Montana, but super backup Steve Young, waiting patiently in the shadows, filled in marvelously when Super Joe was injured. The team's main running threat was still Roger Craig, who shared the backfield with Tom Rathman.

It was at receiver that the 49ers had been transformed. Jerry Rice, in his fourth pro season, was already being called the best all-around pass catcher in history. The constant double-teams he drew left the field open for Craig and Rathman, as well as wideouts John Taylor and Mike Wilson and tight end John Frank. The hard-hitting San Francisco defense, led again by Ronnie Lott, was especially good down the stretch, when the 49ers faced several must-win games in December.

The Bengals' road to the Super Bowl started in the division basement, where they

had finished the season before. Just as Forrest Gregg had done in 1981, Sam Wyche found the right mix for his talented troops in 1988 and went from worst to first in just one season. The main reason was quarterback Boomer Esiason. After three years as a good starting quarterback, he became a great one, leading the AFC with 28 touchdowns and finishing as the top-ranked passer in all of football. Esiason's favorite targets were receivers Eddie Brown and Tim McGee, running back James Brooks, and tight end Rodney Holman. The offense got a further boost from 240-pound (110-kg) fullback Ickey Woods, a rookie out of the University of Nevada-Las Vegas, who celebrated each of his 15 touchdowns with a bizarre dance that he called the "Ickey Shuffle." The Cincinnati defense was rock-hard, with nose tackle Tim Krumrie and backs Eric Thomas and David Fulcher setting the tone.

The Cincinnati Bengals were relaxed and loose heading into Super Bowl XXIII, but it would be the 49ers who played best under pressure.

AS SEEN ON TV

Super Bowl XXIII marked a beginning and an end for pro football. It was the final NFL game in the brilliant career of San Francisco coach Bill Walsh. It also was the game that thrust receiver Jerry Rice into the national spotlight. How the two came together is one of the game's most unusual stories.

Late one Saturday in the fall of 1984, Bill Walsh returned to his hotel room and clicked on the TV. He had finished his final meeting for the next day's game against the Houston Oilers and was getting ready to turn in for the night. As was his habit, he began channel surfing for highlights from that day's college games. Suddenly he saw a player who took his breath away.

Jerry Rice, an unknown pass catcher from tiny Mississippi Valley State University, seemed to be playing the game at a different speed than everyone else on the

Jerry Rice finds the end zone against the Bengals. Passed over by 15 NFL teams during the 1985 draft, he ended up dominating his first Super Bowl, then went on to enjoy a record-breaking career.

field. Walsh watched Rice score five touchdowns and determined at that very moment that if the 49ers did not draft this young man, he might soon be scoring touchdowns against San Francisco.

In the months that followed, the 49ers launched a quiet but thorough investigation into Rice. They could not afford to tip their hand because they had the 28th pick in the draft. If other teams found out that they wanted Rice, they would surely grab him. That is how highly regarded San Francisco's scouting department was.

Rice had grown up in the tiny town of Crawford, Mississippi. His father, Joe, was a mason. During school breaks and summer vacations, Rice and his brothers helped his father on the job. When a project reached the second story, scaffolding was erected to support a new pile of bricks. The Rice boys would throw the bricks up one at a time, and young Jerry would catch and stack them. Soon Jerry could catch two bricks thrown simultaneously. Then three. Then four. His concentration and hand-eye coordination were phenomenal.

Despite his obvious receiving skills, Rice did not play football until his sophomore year in high school. The school principal, Ezell Wicks, caught him cutting class one day. Rice panicked and ran. Wicks had never seen a student move so fast. The next day, the speedy sophomore was summoned to the principal's office, where he learned that part of his punishment included reporting to the school football coach.

Rice was an instant star, and he soon realized that football was his ticket to an education. He accepted a scholarship to nearby MVSU, where he worked hard in the classroom and even harder on the football field. That is what convinced the 49ers to draft him in the first round. Players from small schools are hard to judge because they do not face top competition, but Walsh and his staff knew that Rice would practice and learn whatever it took to become a superstar in the NFL.

On draft day, the 49ers had only one worry. They knew the Dallas Cowboys (who picked 17th) were looking for receivers. Terrified that Dallas had discovered Rice, too, the team made a trade with the Patriots (who owned the number 16 pick) to move ahead of the Cowboys. Everyone at the draft wondered who San Francisco had gone to such trouble to secure. When Rice's name was announced, the experts were stumped. The 49ers' fans wondered if Walsh had lost his mind.

Walsh just smiled. He knew what he had.

By his second season, Rice was the NFL's top receiver. In 1987, he set a new mark for touchdown catches despite playing in just 12 games. In 1988, he overcame a sore ankle to dominate San Francisco's playoff opponents. Then he caught 11 passes for 215 yards in Super Bowl XXIII to earn MVP honors. Rice, who surpassed the 20,000-yard mark in 2001, is regarded as the best receiver ever to play in the NFL. Some even considered him the best football player in history.

CHAPTER 4

THE 1990s

Super Bowl XXIV
January 28, 1990
(1989 Season)
San Francisco 49ers (NFC)
vs. Denver Broncos (AFC)

The 49ers returned to the Super Bowl with a new coach, George Seifert. For years he had served as Bill Walsh's trusted aide and defensive guru. Now Seifert had to fill Walsh's shoes, and that meant nothing less than winning the big game. Not since Don Shula (and his "quest for perfection") had a coach felt as much pressure to win. Standing in his path were John Elway and the Denver Broncos, back for a third shot at football's ultimate prize.

For the first time since Elway joined the Broncos, they did not live and die by his strong right arm. An aggressive new defense and a run-oriented offense brought the Broncos the AFC crown in what was, for Elway, an off year. Rookie Bobby Humphrey, a star at Alabama, came into camp and won the starting halfback job. He finished with 1,151 yards, and Sammy Winder, now the team's fullback, gained another 351. The defense, under new assistant Wade Phillips, made enormous strides with the addition of several key free agents and the arrival of rookie

Steve Atwater, one of the hardest hitting safeties anyone had ever seen.

Under their new, defense-oriented head coach, the 49ers put together an awesome offense. Joe Montana completed more than 70 percent of his passes, tossed 28 touchdowns, and threw only 8 interceptions. Jerry Rice caught 82 balls, scored 17 times, and led the league with more than 1,400 receiving yards. John Taylor, whose catch won Super Bowl XXIII, emerged at age 27 as a 60-catch, 10-touchdown receiver. The offensive line hobbled through injuries at times, but that barely affected Roger Craig, who ran for over 1,000 yards. Fullback Tom Rathman turned in another fine season, with 73 catches out of the backfield. As always, the San Francisco defense was rock steady.

Many of the experts had the Broncos as two-touchdown underdogs in this game. Less than 5 minutes into the opening quarter, it was easy to see why. On San Francisco's first series, Montana sliced right through the Denver defense and threw a 20-yard pass to Rice for the game's first touchdown. The Broncos surprised the 49ers by coming right back with a scoring drive of their own to make the score 7-3. Seifert and his staff had expected Denver to use a ball-control offense. By handing off to Humphrey and Winder, Elway would be able to build long drives. This in turn would keep San Francisco's dangerous offense off the field. Instead, Elway was looking to open up the field by moving around in the pocket and hitting his receivers.

Watching from the sideline, Montana, Rice, and Taylor were getting excited. If a shootout was what Dan Reeves and the Broncos wanted, that is what they would get! Montana directed another quick drive and hit Brent Jones for a 7-yard score. Mike Cofer missed the extra point, making it 13-3. Elway kept throwing for the Broncos, but he was not playing his "A game" on this day. To make matters worse, Humphrey was nursing a rib injury that limited his effectiveness as a runner. The Broncos were in deep trouble.

The 49ers kept rolling in the second quarter. They upped the score to 20-3 on a 1-yard plunge by Rathman and then added another seven points to their lead when Montana found Rice with a 38-yard scoring pass. The teams were separated by 24 points when they went into the locker room at halftime.

Two quarters later, they were separated by 45 points. The Broncos managed just one touchdown in the second half—an Elway keeper from 3 yards out. Before that, however, Montana hit Rice with a 28-yard touchdown pass and Taylor with a 35-yard scoring strike.

Up 41-10, the 49ers kept pouring it on. Trying to run out the clock, Montana concentrated on handing off to Craig and Rathman. This produced a 75-yard touchdown drive, and Rathman found the end zone for a second time at the start of the fourth quarter. The final points came after Elway

The 49ers proved they deserved consideration as one of football's all-time great dynasties after dismantling the Broncos in Super Bowl XXIV. Versatile big-play defenders like Danny Stubbs (#96) were the unsung heroes of a team more famous for its offense.

SUPER JOE

Joe Montana was named MVP in three of his team's four Super Bowl victories. At his best in the big games, he earned the nickname "Super Joe."

With his outstanding performance in Super Bowl XXIV, Joe Montana established himself as the greatest big-game quarterback in NFL history. Four times he reached the Super Bowl, and four times he won. Heading into this contest, the thirty-three-year-old had prevailed in a tight defensive battle (Super Bowl XVI), triumphed in a shoot-out with a record-setting passer (Super Bowl XIX), and engineered an unforgettable come-from-behind victory (Super Bowl XXIII). Now he faced rifle-armed John Elway and an excellent defense.

Montana responded by producing a good old-fashioned blowout. In the first half, he led the 49ers to four touchdowns against a team that had allowed four touchdowns in an entire game only once all year. Montana kept it up in the second half, producing four more touchdowns to humble the Broncos 55-10. For the third time, Super Joe was named Super Bowl MVP.

Montana's final Super Bowl numbers are awe-inspiring. In four games he completed 83 passes for 1,142 yards and 11 touchdowns. He did not throw a single interception, and he once connected on 13 passes in a row. All of these numbers are Super Bowl records. So is his 127.8 quarterback rating for the four games. That may be the most amazing number of all. No quarterback has come close to that mark against regular-season opponents. Montana achieved it against a quartet of AFC champions.

fumbled on Denver's next possession. Daniel Stubbs returned it to the 1-yard line before being tackled. Craig took it in from there to make the final score 55-10.

```
49ers 55
Broncos 10
        Best Player: Joe Montana
```

Super Bowl XXV
January 12, 1991
(1990 Season)
New York Giants (NFC)
vs. Buffalo Bills (AFC)

For several years, the Buffalo Bills had been on the verge of winning it all in the AFC. They had an excellent defense, a solid passing game, a superstar runner, and a good coach. Their trip to Super Bowl XXV was viewed as the final step in a long process. The New York Giants had the excellent defense and the good coach, but they lacked the offensive weapons of the Bills. Their rise to the top of the NFC required a little luck—specifically, the bad luck of their opponents. The 49ers were on their way to a third straight Super Bowl when they ran into the New Yorkers in the conference championship. San Francisco allowed no touchdowns all game and held a solid lead with just a few minutes to go. When the final whistle blew, they not only had lost the game but also had lost their great quarterback, Joe Montana, to a devastating arm injury. What misery would the Giants visit upon the favored Bills in the Super Bowl? Millions tuned in to find out.

Lawrence Taylor, veteran leader of the New York defense, was bad luck for everyone during the year. He played with his usual abandon, and the Giants got superb seasons from Leonard Marshall, Pepper Johnson, Mark Collins, and Everson Walls. The offense had just enough to get the job done, but not much more. Coach Bill Parcells told his team they could make it to the Super Bowl, but they would have to be practically perfect. Quarterback Phil Simms responded with his best season ever, throwing just 4 interceptions in 311 attempts. The Giants as a team made just 14 turnovers during the year, which shattered the NFL record for mistake-free football. Veteran Ottis Anderson, rookie Rodney Hampton, and little Dave Meggett gave the team good options in the backfield, while tight end Mark Bavaro and wideouts Steven Baker and Mark Ingram made clutch catches. The secret to the success of the offense was its massive front line.

Marv Levy's Bills breezed through their season. They had stars everywhere. Jim Kelly was the AFC's top-ranked passer; Thurman Thomas was its most durable and productive running back; Andre Reed and James Lofton were two of its best receivers; and Howard Ballard, Jim Ritcher, and Kent Hull were tremendous offensive linemen. On the other side of the football, the Bills boasted superstars Bruce Smith, Cornelius Bennett, Shane Conlan, and Darryl Talley. The only knock on Buffalo was that Levy was too conservative in the use of his stars. The coach silenced his critics in the playoffs when he unleashed his offense on the Dolphins and the Raiders and scored a combined 95 points.

The Giants knew they were up against big odds. Simms, who was injured late in the year, would not be able to play. Backup Jeff Hostetler, who had played well in his place, would be in command. By game time, Coach Parcells and his staff had determined that there was just one formula for winning. On offense, they had to eat up the clock with long, ball-controlling drives; on defense, they had to tackle Thomas and Reed hard to tire them out.

The strategy got off to a great start when the Giants stuffed the Bills on their first series, then came back with an 11-play drive that resulted in a field goal by Matt Bahr, who was playing in the Super Bowl with his third team. The Bills came back right away, as Kelly and Lofton burned the Giants with a 61-yard pass play. New York held its ground and kept Kelly out of the end zone, and Buffalo had to settle for a Scott Norwood field goal and a 3-3 tie.

The Bills, however, would not be denied. Their game plan was simple: overwhelm the outmanned Giants. This they did in the second quarter with a 12-play drive that ended in a 1-yard touchdown by fullback Don Smith. Later in the period, the Bills pinned the Giants against their own goal line, and Bruce Smith tackled Hostetler in the end zone for a safety to make the score 12-3.

The Giants showed their resilience right before the half. With a little less than 4 minutes left, they got the ball on their own 13-yard line and marched all the way down the field. Hostetler made a nice throw to Baker for a touchdown, cutting the deficit to 12-10.

In the locker room, Parcells tried to focus his troops. The younger defensive players needed to calm down, or Kelly and Thomas would cut them to ribbons in the second half. The offense was doing just fine. The Bills were quietly confident. Thomas was the best player on the field;

Kelly was the better quarterback; and it would only be a matter of time before their defense destroyed the inexperienced Hostetler.

The Giants took the second-half kickoff and started to grind out the yards. Running behind Jumbo Elliott, Bart Oates, William Roberts, and the rest of the massive front line, Anderson smashed his way for good gains. Meggett, working out of the backfield, made a couple of clutch receptions. The play of the drive was made by Ingram, who broke four tackles after catching a short pass and made a critical first down. After shearing nearly 10 minutes off the clock, the Giants finally found the end zone and took a 17-12 lead.

It had been nearly an hour since the Buffalo offense had been on the field, but that slowed them down for only a few plays. Once they regained their rhythm, they tore right through the Giants, and Thomas scored on a magnificent 31-yard run. The fourth quarter began with the Bills leading 19-17.

This is when the first bit of bad luck struck Buffalo. Kelly had scored so quickly after the Giants' long drive that the Buffalo defense was still gasping for air when it had to retake the field. Now New York's big front line pounded the Bills, moving them slowly backward until they were within field-goal range. Bahr came on again and converted a 21-yard kick to put the Giants up 20-19.

With half a quarter to go, the Bills were confident they could win. Their offense had moved with ease all day against the Giants, and all they needed here was a field goal. After their first drive failed, the Bills got the ball back with a couple of minutes left. Kelly executed his "hurry-up" offense

HOLD EVERYTHING!

The key to New York's remarkable Super Bowl run was their uncanny ability to limit turnovers in close games. During the regular season, the Giants lost the ball only 14 times. This is by far the best mark in NFL history. When they did commit a turnover, often it came when a win was already assured—as in their 31-3 victory over the Chicago Bears during the playoffs.

Many feel that the key play for the Giants in Super Bowl XXV was made by Jeff Hostetler when he was tackled by the Buffalo Bills for a safety. The play occurred in the second quarter, with the New Yorkers pinned on their own 7-yard line. Hostetler dropped back to pass, then tripped over running back Ottis Anderson's foot. The quarterback fell down in the end zone and barely scrambled to his feet before Bruce Smith came crashing into him.

Smith, who outweighed Hostetler by 70 pounds (32 kg) and had arms like steel girders, tried desperately to strip the ball from his hands. Hostetler endured the punishment and somehow held on to the football. The safety gave Buffalo a 12-3 lead. A fumble recovery, however, would have put the Bills up 17-3 and altered the entire complexion of the game. The play by Hostetler—one of the toughest and most determined quarterbacks ever—was typical of the little things that brought New York a most unlikely and unexpected championship that season.

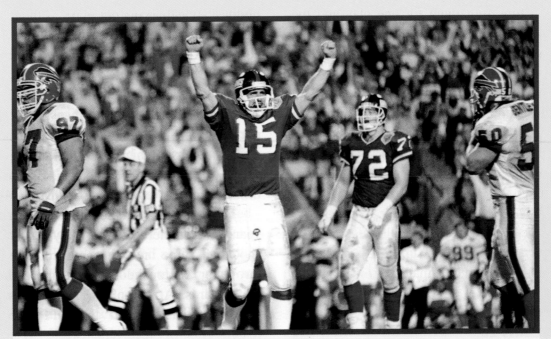

Jeff Hostetler typified the hard-nosed style of the 1990 New York Giants.

was sacked and lost the football. Defensive end Jimmie Jones picked it out of the air and fell over the goal line from 2 yards out. Dallas now led 14-7.

Marv Levy had warned his players not to make errors like this. The Cowboys were an energetic and emotional team that thrived on sudden swings of momentum. This was exactly what Levy was talking about. The Bills regrouped and added a field goal in the second quarter, but everyone in the Rose Bowl could sense that the Cowboys were about to explode.

The play that lit the fuse was another mistake by Kelly. After directing a march down to the Dallas goal line, the Buffalo quarterback threw a fourth-down pass that was intercepted in the end zone. Instead of having a 17-14 lead and control of the game, the Bills were down 14-10 and running for their lives. Aikman came right down the field for a touchdown with a beautiful pass to Irvin. Up 21-10, Aikman and Irvin took another Buffalo turnover and converted it into a touchdown for a 28-10 halftime lead.

President Bill Clinton, flanked by coach Jimmy Johnson and team owner Jerry Jones, welcomes the Cowboys to the White House after their victory in Super Bowl XXVII.

LITTLE VICTORY

The most replayed moment of Dallas's 52-17 blowout in Super Bowl XXVII was a small moment of triumph for the Buffalo Bills. With the fourth quarter ticking away and the Cowboys in complete control, the Bills were playing for pride. When quarterback Frank Reich was sacked and the ball tumbled to the turf, it looked like they were in for one more dose of humiliation.

Leon Lett, the Cowboys' 6-foot-6 (1.98-m), 300-pound (136-km) defensive tackle, scooped up the ball and headed toward the end zone. With no one between himself and the goal line, he was certain he would score a Super Bowl touchdown—the ultimate accomplishment for a defensive lineman. With 10 yards to go, Lett started celebrating his good fortune. He shifted the ball into his outstretched palm, no doubt preparing for a spectacular spike.

The moment he saw the loose ball, Buffalo's Don Beebe—one of Reich's receivers—began sprinting back to the play. With the crowd cheering and visions of stardom dancing in his head, the thundering Lett never heard Beebe, the smallest man on the field, coming up behind him.

Just before Lett crossed the goal line, Beebe lunged forward and knocked the ball loose to prevent a touchdown. Realizing he was now the biggest jerk on the field, Lett could do little more than slink to the Dallas sideline. Beebe, on the other hand, got a huge pat on the back from his teammates. His hustle had restored their spirits on a day when there was little to celebrate.

Buffalo's Don Beebe zeroes in on the football as Leon Lett begins his celebration a few yards short of the end zone.

There was not much to say in the Buffalo locker room. The Bills had lost control of the game, and Kelly's knee hurt too much to continue. Reich had already produced one postseason miracle; no one expected him to do it again.

Dallas opened the scoring in the third quarter with a 20-yard field goal by Lin Elliot. Trailing 31-10, Reich went to work and hit wide receiver Don Beebe for a long touchdown. That was the last of the scoring for the Bills, who played the rest of the way like the badly beaten team that they were.

Meanwhile, the Cowboys continued to pour it on. In the final period, Aikman connected with Alvin Harper on a 45-yard touchdown play, and 2 minutes later Smith scored on a 10-yard run to make the score 45-17. The game ended 52-17 after linebacker Ken Norton scooped up a fumble by Reich and raced into the end zone. It was Buffalo's ninth turnover of the game.

The Bills had no one to blame but themselves. They were the experienced team. They had the game within their grasp. After going 0-for-3 in Super Bowls, the fans were getting tired of saying "Wait 'til next year."

**Cowboys 52
Bills 17
Best Player: Troy Aikman**

Super Bowl XXVIII
January 30, 1994
(1993 Season)
Dallas Cowboys (NFC)
vs. Buffalo Bills (AFC)

For the first time, a Super Bowl featured a replay of the previous year's game. The Cowboys and the Bills were well acquainted by now. After blowing out Buffalo in Super Bowl XXVII, Dallas lost to the Bills in the second week of the 1993 season. It was little consolation for Buffalo, however. The Cowboys had been without the services of Emmitt Smith, who was holding out for a better contract. Smith got his money soon after, and then he led Dallas to 12 wins over the final 14 games. When the two teams took the field again for their Super Bowl rematch, they were both at full strength.

Dallas was firing on all cylinders on both offense and defense. Troy Aikman threw just 6 interceptions in nearly 400 pass attempts; Michael Irvin caught 88 balls; and Alvin Harper developed into a big-play receiver, averaging a league-high 21.6 yards per catch. Smith rushed for 1,486 yards despite missing the first two weeks, and he was named NFL MVP. The Cowboy defense was led by a formidable front line that included Leon Lett, Russell Maryland, Charles Haley, Tony Tolbert, and Tony Casillas. Dallas's depth was the key to its success. Like every team, the Cowboys suffered key injuries during the year—but Jimmy Johnson always had a fresh and talented body to plug the hole.

Buffalo, meanwhile, had become a team known as much for its defense as for its offense. The veteran core of Bruce Smith, Darryl Talley, and Cornelius Bennett led a unit that made big plays when it had to. Only once during the season did an opponent score more than three touchdowns on the Bills, who allowed just 242 points all year. Jim Kelly, recovered from his knee injury, threw for more than 3,000 yards, and Thurman Thomas led the AFC again with 1,315, but a rash of turnovers made a lot of easy wins into nail-biters. As Levy reminded his troops, mistakes against the Cowboys would be deadly.

Dallas did have some concerns heading into Super Bowl XXVIII. The Bills were using a three-receiver offense, which would force Johnson to sit a lineman or a linebacker and to use an extra defensive back instead. This was the defense's weakest point. Also, Smith had an aching shoulder, and it was unclear how much pain he could bear once the Bills started tackling him.

In the first quarter, the two teams prodded and probed each other. Both offenses moved the ball, but neither could get into the end zone. After 15 minutes, the score was 6-3 in favor of the Cowboys. The second quarter belonged to the Bills. Kelly mastered the Dallas defense and engineered a long touchdown drive to grab a 10-6 lead. Then he got the team deep into enemy territory again for another field goal. The Buffalo defense, meanwhile, held Aikman & Co. in check. The Bills led 13-6 at halftime.

In the locker room, the Cowboys looked at one another in disbelief. After their blowout of the Bills the year before, they secretly had assumed this game would be easy. Dallas had done a good job slowing Thomas down, but Kelly was killing them with his passing. Levy and his staff had done an excellent scouting job, and now it was up to Dallas to make the correct adjustment. Otherwise, the game would slip away.

The Bills took the second-half kickoff and once again began advancing on the Cowboys. Dallas fans grew nervous, as Buffalo seemed destined for another score. Then, on a handoff to Thomas, Lett stripped the ball. James Washington—the fifth pass defender Johnson had been forced to use—

grabbed it and ran 46 yards for a touchdown to tie the score at 13-13. As Levy feared, the turnover seemed to wake up the Cowboys. On their next possession, Dallas's offensive line punched holes in the Buffalo defense as Smith carried the ball seven times on an eight-play scoring drive. Dallas held a 20-13 lead as the fourth quarter began.

Kelly, still throwing well, tried to even the count. He guided his team into scoring position, then threw a bad pass that was picked off by Washington, the unexpected hero of the day. Now Dallas really poured

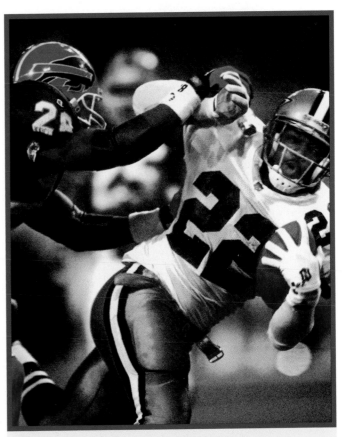

Emmitt Smith sheds a Buffalo tackler in Super Bowl XXVIII. He turned in an MVP performance despite a painful shoulder injury.

BUILDING BLOCKS

Quarterback Troy Aikman was the centerpiece in the rebuilding strategy of the Dallas Cowboys. He retired with two Super Bowl rings and more than 30,000 career passing yards.

The four keys to a dominant offensive football team are a steady offensive line, a tough and talented quarterback, a running game with power and speed, and sure-handed, big-play receivers. The number of teams that have had this combination can be counted on one hand. In the 1950s, the Cleveland Browns had it, and they won three NFL championships. In the 1960s, the Green Bay Packers had it, and they won five league titles as well as the first two Super Bowls. In the 1970s, the Pittsburgh Steelers had it, and they won four Super Bowls. In the late 1980s, the San Francisco 49ers had it, and they won the big game twice. In the early 1990s, the Dallas Cowboys built a team on these same principles and won it all in 1993 and 1994.

Of all these super teams, only the Cowboys had to start from scratch. Under Coach Tom Landry in the 1980s, the team clung to its veterans too long, drafted poorly, and got progressively worse. When Jimmy Johnson was hired in 1989, he swept out the old-timers and began looking for building blocks. He found them in rookies Darryl Johnston and Troy Aikman, to whom he handed starting jobs. The new coach also had receiver Michael Irvin, whom he had coached in college. Johnson liked Irvin's hunger for winning and decided to make him Aikman's primary target.

After suffering through a 1-15 season, the Cowboys continued to add pieces to the puzzle. Draft pick Emmitt Smith gave Dallas a second good runner, and free agent Jay Novacek gave Aikman a glue-fingered tight end. The Cowboys improved to 7-9, and only injuries to Aikman and Irvin kept them out of the playoffs.

In 1991, Johnson drafted a third receiver, Alvin Harper, and the offensive line began coming together. Veterans Nate Newton and Mark Tuinei, as well as youngsters Erik Williams and Mark Stepnoski, all developed into top blockers. The only hole left to plug was the defense, which gave up 310 points in '91—86 more than the division-winning Redskins.

In 1992, the Cowboys' defense finally came together, and completely shut down enemy ground attacks. Veterans Charles Haley and Tony Casillas anchored a line that included young stars Russell Maryland, Leon Lett, and Tony Tolbert. The linebacking corps featured dynamic Ken Norton, while the secondary was led by gung-ho veteran Billy Bates.

During the 1992 and 1993 seasons, the Cowboys won 25 of 32 regular season games and swept all six of their postseason contests in convincing fashion. In the team's two Super Bowls victories (1993 and 1994), the Cowboys outscored the Buffalo Bills by a total of 52 points.

Although fans will best remember the exploits of Aikman, Irvin, and Smith, any coach will tell you that Dallas's amazing return to the top of football was a classic team effort.

it on. Another drive resulted in Smith's second touchdown of the day, and kicker Eddie Murray later booted his third field goal.

The score was 30-13, and Buffalo was finished. Forced to pass on nearly every play, Kelly was an easy target for the Dallas pass rush, and he failed to put a single point on the board. The Dallas Cowboys had their fourth Super Bowl win, equaling the record of the Steelers and the 49ers.

As for the Bills, they had an unwanted record all to themselves: four Super Bowls, four losses. Also for the fourth time, victory had been within their grasp. A collection of stars that fans hoped would one day be called the team of the 1990s instead became the NFL's biggest joke.

> **Cowboys 30**
> **Bills 13**
> Best Player: Emmitt Smith

Super Bowl XXIX
January 29, 1995
(1994 Season)
San Francisco 49ers (NFC)
vs. San Diego Chargers (AFC)

Steve Young was a man looking for respect. After taking over for Joe Montana in 1992, he had done everything a quarterback could do except win a Super Bowl for the 49ers. Now he was expected to win. San Francisco's opponent, the San Diego Chargers, were expected to lose—but then, this was the same bunch that had been picked to finish last in the AFC West. Still big underdogs in Super Bowl XXIX, the Chargers were a team that could not be taken lightly.

The Chargers specialized in catching the enemy off-guard. Under coach Bobby Ross, they sneaked up on the rest of the AFC by winning their first six games and then hung on to fend off the Chiefs and the Raiders. Twice in the playoffs they came from behind to beat superior teams. The Charger offense was powered by resourceful Stan Humphries, a veteran quarterback whose talents meshed perfectly with those of Natrone Means, a 250-pound (113-kg) rookie running back. This one-two punch—plus a trio of sure-handed wide receivers—gave San Diego enough points to let its defense win games. The key tacklers for the Chargers were linebacker Junior Seau and end Leslie O'Neal. They led a unit that was murder against the run and made big plays against the pass. Five times during the season, a Charger defensive back turned an interception into a touchdown.

The San Diego defense would be put to the test against the 49ers. Since becoming the starter, Young had put up quarterback ratings in the 100s and had led the league in touchdown throws for three straight seasons. Jerry Rice, in his prime, caught 112 balls for 1,499 yards and 13 touchdowns in 1994. Wideout John Taylor, tight end Brent Jones, and running back Ricky Watters combined for 156 receptions and another 25 touchdowns. The San Francisco defense blended young studs like Dana Stubblefield, Bryant Young, and Merton Hanks with old pros like Richard Dent, Charles Mann, Tim Harris, and Deion Sanders.

The Chargers kicked off to begin the game, and within 90 seconds the 49ers had put to rest any thought that their passing game would be contained. On the third play of the game, Young hit Rice going down the

THE 1990s • 109

middle, and he went all the way for a 44-yard touchdown. No one had ever scored that quickly in a Super Bowl.

The 49ers appeared to be in a hurry during the whole game. On their next possession, Young connected with Watters across the middle, and for the second time in 5 minutes the Chargers watched helplessly as San Francisco scored a long touchdown. Hoping to bring the game under control, Humphries and Means put together a long, conservative drive that ended with Means tumbling into the end zone from 1 yard out. San Diego trailed 14-7.

In the second quarter, Young matched Humphries's feat with a long drive of his own. With the ball on the 5-yard line, he called William Floyd's number. With San Diego covering every receiver, Young tossed the ball to the burly fullback for a touchdown and a 21-7 lead. Young did it again a few minutes later, capping off a drive with an 8-yard scoring pass to Watters to put the 49ers up 28-7. The half ended 28-10 after Jon Carney booted a late field goal for the Chargers.

In the locker room, coach George Seifert reminded the 49ers to have fun but to take the second half seriously. Play hard, he told them, and you'll have nothing to worry about. Ross, meanwhile, did not know what to tell his players.

The second half began just like the first. The 49ers moved down the field with ease against the Chargers. This time Watters scored on the ground, from 15 yards away. His third touchdown of the day, it tied a Super Bowl record. Several minutes later, Young found his favorite receiver, Rice, for yet another score to give his team a 42-10 advantage. The Chargers got Rice's seven points back on the kickoff when Andre

After years as an understudy to Joe Montana, Steve Young finally emerged as a winner in his own right.

Coleman made a 98-yard return, but it was too late.

In the final period, each team embarked on one last scoring drive. The final score was 49-26, but the game did not even seem that close.

49ers 49
Chargers 26
  Best Player: Steve Young

YOUNG AND RESTLESS

For Steve Young, the what-ifs don't mean a thing anymore. After winning Super Bowl XXIX, there was nothing left for him to accomplish as a quarterback. Before this victory, however, Young's career was one of questionable choices and bad luck.

Coming out of high school, Young was coveted by many of the top colleges. He had the size of a fullback, the speed of a halfback, and the instincts of a quarterback. He turned everyone down—including powerhouse Notre Dame—because he wanted to be a passer, not a runner. Young ended up at Brigham Young University (named after his great-great-great-grandfather), where it took him more than a year to work his way up to the starting job.

Once in command, Young was fantastic. He threw for 7,733 yards and 56 touchdowns in just 28 college games. In 1984, he was the first-round selection of the Tampa Bay Buccaneers. Instead of signing with the NFL, however, Young chose to join the fledgling United States Football League. He was promised tens of millions of dollars (most of which he never received) and great pass protection (which he rarely got).

After the USFL folded, Young joined Tampa Bay, where he spent two seasons running for his life. The pass blocking was terrible, and the guys chasing him in the NFL were a lot bigger and meaner than in the USFL. Young lucked out when he was traded to the San Francisco 49ers in 1987. Coach Bill Walsh ran an offense tailor-

Super Bowl XXX
January 28, 1996
(1995 Season)
Dallas Cowboys (NFC)
vs. Pittsburgh Steelers (AFC)

Sometimes a football coach can make the difference between a winning season and a losing one. Sometimes he makes no difference at all. The Dallas Cowboys were a group of veteran stars who knew how to win, so when Jimmy Johnson was replaced with college coach Barry Switzer, the Cowboys barely missed a beat. The Pittsburgh Steelers hoped that the lack of an experienced pro coach would hurt Dallas in the Super Bowl. They also hoped that their own

coach, fiery Bill Cowher, would devise a plan to upset the favored Cowboys. He had gotten the Steelers to the big game despite losing his two top players from the year before. If they could get this far, maybe they could go all the way.

This would not be an easy task. Troy Aikman, Emmitt Smith, and Michael Irvin made the Cowboys extremely hard to beat in big games. During the 1995 season, Aikman threw for 3,304 yards and only 7 interceptions; Smith set a new league mark with 25 rushing touchdowns; Irvin caught 11 touchdown passes. Add to this trio superstar cornerback Deion "Prime Time" Sanders, and Dallas seemed to hold all the cards in Super Bowl XXX. Prime Time

made for his skills, and as long as he was willing to sit on the bench for a couple of seasons, Young could expect great things when his time came.

Four years later, his time still had not come. Young was now close to 30 years old, and he was still a benchwarmer behind Joe Montana. Given a chance to leave via free agency, Young decided to stay. Many questioned his judgment; Montana looked like he might go on forever.

Finally, in 1992, Montana moved on, and Young was inserted as San Francisco's starter. He had one of the greatest seasons ever, but the aging 49ers lost to the up-and-coming Cowboys in the NFC championship game. Young was criticized for his inability to convert several key third-down plays and for throwing two interceptions.

In 1993, Young had an even better year, with 4,023 passing yards—but again he lost to the Cowboys. This defeat hurt even more, for Dallas coach Jimmy Johnson had brashly guaranteed a Cowboys victory before the game.

With age creeping up on Young and San Francisco fans growing impatient, it was time to win or to get out of town. Young responded with what many consider to be the best all-around season in history. He completed an astounding 70.3 percent of his passes for 3,969 yards and 35 touchdowns. In 461 attempts, he threw just 10 interceptions. Young's quarterback rating of 112.8 has never been equaled.

Against the Chargers in the Super Bowl, Young was simply magnificent. After so many years of being second-guessed, Young finally was everyone's choice for the top player in football.

played on both sides of the football in 1995, lining up at receiver on several plays. His greatest impact was on defense, where he teamed with Darren Woodson to give the Cowboys the league's top pass-defense tandem. This forced enemy quarterbacks to throw in the direction of cornerback Larry Brown and safety Brock Marion, who were no slouches either—in fact, they intercepted a total of 12 passes to only 4 for Sanders and Woodson.

The man charged with solving the Dallas defense was quarterback Neil O'Donnell, who was having his best year as a passer. With O'Donnell and a group of receivers that included Yancey Thigpen, Andre Hastings, and Ernie Mills, the Steelers were able to rely less on their ground attack. And then there was rookie Kordell Stewart, who made big plays at running back, receiver, and quarterback. The timing could not have been better, as running back Barry Foster—the team's best offensive player—was out for the season. Pittsburgh's best defensive player, Rod Woodson, was lost to injury in the season's first game. Picking up the slack were Greg Lloyd, Kevin Greene, and Levon Kirkland—the AFC's top linebacking trio—along with end Ray Seals and cornerbacks Willie Williams and Carnell Lake.

With both teams featuring excellent secondaries, it was hard to imagine that this Super Bowl would be won through the air.

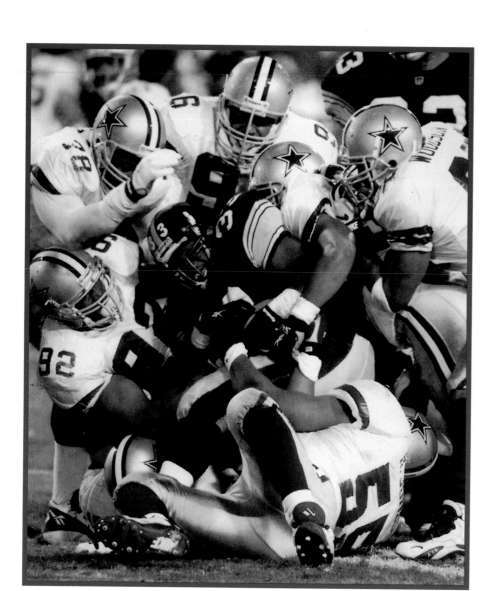

Pittsburgh running back Bam Morris disappears in a swarm of Dallas tacklers during Super Bowl XXX.

It could, however, be lost through the air. Sticking to short passes and hard running by Smith, Aikman followed this logic and directed the Cowboys to two scores in the first quarter to give his team a 10-0 lead. Early in the second period, the Cowboys added another field goal, making the score 13-0.

After probing the Dallas secondary with little success, O'Donnell finally put together a drive in the second quarter. The Steelers moved to the 6-yard line, and O'Donnell found Thigpen open in the end zone. The score was now Dallas 13, Pittsburgh 7.

The late score gave the Steelers a big boost. Cowher assured his players at halftime that they could win. Although Dallas had scored three times, he felt the defense was doing an excellent job against Smith and Irvin. In fact, the only "bad" play Pittsburgh had allowed was a 47-yard completion to Sanders. If the Steelers could continue this effort in the second half, they had a very real chance at victory. The Cowboys recognized that they were having trouble with the Pittsburgh defense but felt that O'Donnell was playing right into their

UNHAPPY HOLLIDAY

Right before the interception that killed Pittsburgh's chances to win Super Bowl XXX, the Steelers looked like certain winners. That single play turned the game around. Why, Pittsburgh fans are still wondering, did Neil O'Donnell throw the ball so accurately into the arms of Dallas's Larry Brown? Did he mistake him for a teammate? Did Brown have ESP? Why was there not a black-and-yellow jersey within 20 feet (6 m) of the ball?

Corey Holliday knows the answer.

An undrafted receiver out of the University of North Carolina, Holliday joined the Steelers in April 1994. He was cut during training camp, then was re-signed to work on the team's practice squad in November. He never appeared in a game for Pittsburgh that year. In 1995, Holliday was signed and cut on three different occasions. He played in three games and never caught a pass.

Yet there he was, on the field in the Super Bowl, at the most crucial time. O'Donnell called Holliday's number, hoping to fool the Cowboys, who probably had never seen film on Holliday. Unfortunately, Holliday was the one who was fooled. As he burst off the line of scrimmage, he had a brain freeze and ran the wrong route. O'Donnell threw to the spot where his young teammate was supposed to be, then watched helplessly as it floated into enemy arms.

hands. O'Donnell was so concerned with Sanders that he had begun throwing to Larry Brown's side of the field every time he dropped back. If O'Donnell continued this, they would make him pay.

The Steelers opened the third quarter with a strong offensive push. Just when they seemed poised to grab the lead, however, O'Donnell badly under-threw a receiver, and Brown was right there to pick off the pass. He returned it 44 yards, deep into Steeler territory. Two plays later, Smith smashed across the goal line to give the Cowboys a 20-7 lead.

For the rest of the third quarter, the two teams slugged away at each other. The younger, stronger Steelers seemed to gain the upper hand. Early in the fourth quarter, O'Donnell moved the team within field-goal range, and Norm Johnson hit a 46-yarder to narrow the Cowboys' advantage to 20-10. Pittsburgh made another long drive and scored on a 1-yard plunge by Bam Morris.

With a slim 20-17 lead and their momentum all but gone, the Cowboys looked like a team about to lose. But looks can be deceiving. Although tired, Dallas still had experience on its side. When O'Donnell threw his second bad pass of the day, Brown was once again there to intercept it. This time he ran it back to the 6-yard line. Smith found the end zone a few plays later, and the score became Cowboys 27, Steelers 17.

The Dallas defense prevented Pittsburgh from scoring any more points, and that is how the game ended.

Every statistic—except the score—suggested that the Steelers should have won this game. Cowher's plan was a good one, and the Steelers executed it well. Were it not for O'Donnell's two backbreaking interceptions, the outcome could have been dramatically different.

> **Cowboys 27**
> **Steelers 17**
>   Best Player: Larry Brown

Super Bowl XXXI
January 26, 1997
(1996 Season)
Green Bay Packers (NFC) vs.
New England Patriots (AFC)

After nearly three decades, the team that started it all—the Green Bay Packers—finally made it back to the Super Bowl. They faced the New England Patriots, whose coach, Bill Parcells, had engineered a pair of memorable come-from-behind victories with the Giants. Whether he won or lost this game, Parcells would be gone the following season—owner Robert Kraft had already made the decision. The star-studded Packers were the favorites, but no one ever counted out Parcells, who had a young, talented offense and a solid defense.

Vince Lombardi would have loved Brett Favre. No one played harder, and no one wanted to win more. Early in his career, the Green Bay quarterback was hindered by these qualities; too often he tried to win games all by himself, with disastrous

results. Coach Mike Holmgren finally convinced Favre to trust his teammates and to play with a little patience. In 1995, he won the MVP award and led the Packers to the NFC title game. In 1996, he won the MVP again and got the Packers to the Super Bowl. Favre ran an offense similar to the one used by the 49ers. He had a number of weapons at his disposal, including halfback Dorsey Levens; receivers Antonio Freeman, Robert Brooks, and Andre Rison; and tight end Mark Chmura. On defense, the Packers were led by all-time great Reggie White and All-Pro LeRoy Butler.

The Packers' veteran defense would have to contend with several young offensive stars. At 24, Drew Bledsoe was already the best quarterback in New England franchise history. In 1996 he completed 373 passes for 4,086 yards and 27 touchdowns. Running back Curtis Martin, just 23 years old, amassed 1,152 yards on the ground and led the AFC with 14 rushing touchdowns. Receivers Terry Glenn, Ben Coates, and Shawn Jefferson caught a total of 202 passes. And Parcells' old favorite, Dave Meggett, chipped in with more than 1,700 all-purpose yards. The Patriot defense—which featured fast-improving players like Ted Johnson, Willie McGinest, and Lawyer Milloy—committed too many penalties, but they came into the Super Bowl red-hot. The Pats had yet to allow a touchdown in the postseason.

Favre snapped that streak on Green Bay's second play of the game. Recognizing a blitz formation, he barked out a new play at the line and caught the Patriots out of position. Rison went right down the middle of the field, and Favre led him perfectly. The heads-up play was good for a 54-yard touchdown. On the Packers' next posses-

Almost three decades after Green Bay won its first two Super Bowls, Brett Favre led the Packers to their third title.

sion, Chris Jacke booted a 37-yard field goal. And just like that, it was 10-0.

Parcells knew his kids were in danger. He settled Bledsoe down and sent in a series of plays designed to punch holes in the Green Bay defense. Bledsoe executed perfectly, and 79 yards later, 33-year-old Keith Byars found the end zone on a short pass.

Bledsoe got the ball back late in the first period and went to work again. He hit Glenn on a 44-yard play, then connected with Coates for a 4-yard touchdown. The Patriots had surged ahead, 14-10.

Favre responded immediately. On the following series, he hooked up with Free-man on an 81-yard scoring strike, the longest play from scrimmage in Super Bowl history. Back on top, the Packers did not rest. After Jacke added another field goal, Favre extended Green Bay's lead to 27-14 when he scored on a quarterback keeper.

After a wild first half, both coaches had plenty to say to their teams. Holmgren applauded his defense. After allowing the two quick touchdowns, the Packers had seized control of the line of scrimmage. If Favre could score one more touchdown, Holmgren believed, the game would be over. Parcells told his defense to tighten up and made some adjustments designed to keep Favre

MAKING THE GRADE

Desmond Howard was a disappointment as a pro until his explosive performance against the Patriots in Super Bowl XXXI.

The Heisman Trophy is the most prestigious award in college football. Even though it can lead to a handsome pro contract, it does not guarantee success in the pros. For every Heisman-winning superstar, there is an excellent college player who never made the grade in the NFL.

In 1991, Desmond Howard of the University of Michigan won the Heisman and several other awards as the nation's best player. After being selected by the Washington Redskins with the fourth pick in the NFL draft, however, the speedy wide receiver never was able to become a top pass catcher in the pros. In 1992 and 1993 he handled kick-return duties for the Redskins and started just six games as a wideout. In 1994, Howard got a chance to start, but he caught just 40 balls for the 3-13 'Skins.

and Levens in check. He told his offense that there was still time to win, but they would have to regain control of the line so Martin could run.

The Patriots responded to their coach immediately by punishing the Green Bay defensive line and blowing open big holes for Martin. When the linebackers and safeties came in to help, Bledsoe fired quick passes to his receivers. Martin took a handoff on the 18-yard line, broke a tackle, and went in for

the score to make the game 27-21. New England looked like a new team. The Packers looked old.

New England's newfound confidence was crushed when the unthinkable happened. Desmond Howard—a Heisman Trophy-winning wide receiver who had been relegated to kick-return duty—fielded Adam Vinatieri's kickoff on the 1-yard line. He darted up the middle and disappeared into a sea of bodies. As several New En-

Washington left Howard exposed in the NFL expansion draft, and the Jacksonville Jaguars picked him up. Excited about his chance to shine at last, he instead found himself one of many talented receivers on the Jags and made only 26 catches in 7 starts. Jacksonville cut Howard loose after the season, and he signed with the Packers.

Once again, Howard was low man on the totem pole. When he wanted to know why he was not given a chance to start, the Packers told him that he just wasn't good enough. He dropped too many balls, did not run his patterns well, and was not tough enough to play down after down in the NFL. The Packers explained to him that the way he could contribute was to run back punts. Take it or leave it.

Howard took it.

He worked hard to understand the demands of his new job. Although he had returned punts for a time with the Jaguars, he was by no means a specialist. Somewhere in the early part of the season, however, something clicked for Howard, and he became the top return man in football. He fielded 58 punts and returned them an average of 15.1 yards—both tops in the NFL—and scored three thrilling touchdowns. After years of being a dud, Howard was now a bona fide weapon.

Howard's game-breaking 99-yard touchdown against the Patriots in Super Bowl XXXI made the difference not only for the Packers, but also for Howard. Before that moment, he was considered one of the all-time Heisman busts. Now he will be remembered fondly as the man who ensured Green Bay's return to glory.

gland tacklers veered toward him, Howard noticed a seam in the coverage. He bounced off one tackle, regained his balance, and sprinted toward the open area. And just like that, he was gone for a 99-yard touchdown! After Favre passed to Chmura for a two-point conversion, the score was 35-21.

The Patriots were devastated. In a matter of 1 minute, they had gone from kings to paupers. Bledsoe's line could not regain the advantage in the trenches, and the team was out of sync for the rest of the game. The Packers, now energized, slammed the door on New England and ran down the clock. After a scoreless fourth quarter, the Packers were back on top of the football world.

Packers 35
Patriots 21
Best Player: Desmond Howard

Super Bowl XXXII
January 25, 1998
(1997 Season)
Green Bay Packers (NFC)
vs. Denver Broncos (AFC)

Thirty-seven-year-old John Elway had hinted all season that this might be his final NFL campaign. Brett Favre, at the top of his game and supremely confident, believed that his team was on the verge of building a Super Bowl dynasty. Football fans loved both quarterbacks, and many actually planned to root for both in this game. The experts, however, were less concerned about Elway and Favre than they were about the men protecting them. This would be a battle of the lines.

The Packers were intimidating. Besides being the defending NFL champions, they had some serious weight on their defensive line. Reggie White, Gilbert Brown, Santana Dotson, Darius Holland, and Gabe Wilkins collectively tipped the scale at more than 1,500 pounds (680 kg). They simply manhandled their opponents all year. Meanwhile, Favre keyed the Packer attack on the other side of the football. He led the conference in passing yards and threw for an NFL-best 35 touchdowns for the season. Green Bay's offensive line was big and brutal, too. They not only kept enemy pass rushers away from Favre, but also created huge openings for Dorsey Levens, who became one of the NFC's elite runners with 1,435 yards.

The Broncos felt confident that they could contain the Packers on offense. Veterans Neil Smith, Steve Atwater, and Bill Romanowski specialized in making big plays at crucial moments. It was Green Bay's super-sized defenders that most worried Denver coach Mike Shanahan. His offensive line was tiny by NFL standards. It was old, too—most of the guards and tackles were in their 30s. They had walked a fine line all season. With their experience, they bought Elway the time he needed in the pocket. With their agility, they executed crisp blocks to open space for Terrell Davis. The quick and powerful back was superb at squeezing through these openings an instant before they closed. Could they do it against the Packers? The answer would decide the game.

The Broncos were determined not to lose the Super Bowl for the fifth time. They also wanted to end the AFC's embarrassing 13-game losing streak. Not since the Raiders beat the Redskins in 1984 had the NFC lost the championship. Denver hoped to accomplish this by running the football. Coach Shanahan knew that the Packers would have to respect Elway's arm, so they would not be ganging up on his runners. Also, Davis was the kind of player who had given Green Bay problems during the regular season. Mike Holmgren knew this was coming, so he put a big emphasis on grabbing the lead. He wanted to force the Broncos to throw the football.

The Green Bay coach got his wish when Favre marched the team 76 yards on their first series. Favre hit Antonio Freeman with a 22-yard scoring strike to give the Packers a 7-0 lead. Denver came right back, though, when Davis finished off a solid drive with a 1-yard touchdown plunge.

The Broncos broke the tie in the second quarter after cornerback Tyrone Braxton intercepted a Favre pass. Capping a drive to Green Bay's 1-yard line, Elway rolled into the end zone himself. The Broncos went up 17-7 later in the quarter thanks to another turnover. A great tackle by Atwater led to a loose ball, which Neil Smith recovered. The Packers kept the Broncos out of the end zone this time, but Jason Elam was able to hit a 51-yard field goal.

Favre looked to narrow the score and make up for his mistakes. In a long drive that ate up the rest of the second quarter, he brought the Packers within three points when he found tight end Mark Chmura in the end zone.

Rarely had two teams hit the locker room at halftime feeling this good about their chances. Each squad felt it had executed its first-half game plan. Each coach felt that his team could limit its mistakes in the second half. Shanahan was successful with his ground game and saw no reason to alter his approach. Holmgren had detected several soft spots in the Denver defense, and he believed Favre could put a lot of points on the board over the next 30 minutes.

The Packers opened the second half looking to force the action. On Denver's first snap, the defense battered Davis and he coughed up the football. Green Bay recovered, and kicker Ryan Longwell knotted the score moments later at 17-17. Elway restored order with a well-constructed drive that began at his own 8-yard line. Mixing passing and running plays, he moved into Green Bay territory on a clutch catch by receiver Ed McCaffrey. When Denver got close, Davis got the call. He scored his second touchdown of the game for a 24-17 lead.

With each possession more precious than the last, a pair of turnovers greatly magnified the intensity of the game. First, Freeman fumbled Elam's kickoff after Denver's tie-breaking score. Coach Holmgren was furious when the normally sure-handed star lost the handle and veteran Tim McKyer recovered for the Broncos. Moments later, Eugene Robinson read Elway's eyes perfectly and intercepted a pass in the end zone to keep the score close.

Starting from his own 20-yard line, Favre went to work. In just three plays, he maneuvered the Packers into scoring position. On the fourth play of the drive, Freeman made up for his earlier mistake by reeling in a 13-yard touchdown pass. With 13 minutes left in the game, the score was tied again.

For the next several minutes, the Packers and Broncos hammered away at each other, with no one gaining an obvious advantage. Denver's sprightly offensive line was still feeling fresh, however, and the Packers were starting to huff and puff. When Denver got the ball back at midfield following a poor punt by Craig Hentrich, it was time to press this advantage. The Broncos moved swiftly toward the end zone, with Elway himself carrying the ball—and surviving a brutal tackle—on a daring play. Davis finished the short drive with his third touchdown of the game.

Green Bay received the kickoff, and Favre began to pick his way through the Denver defense. Completions to Levens of 22, 13, and then 4 yards got the ball past midfield. Three more plays failed to net a first down, however, and this set up the game-ending play. Favre faded back and struggled to find an open receiver. His desperate pass was batted down by second-year linebacker John Mobley.

The Broncos, one of the most successful franchises in the history of football, finally had something to put in their trophy case. Elway, afraid he would be remembered as the quarterback who couldn't win the big one, was on top of the world.

RIGHT THIS WAY, GENTLEMEN

A defense that purposefully lets an opponent score a touchdown does not belong in the Super Bowl, right? Wrong. At least that is what Green Bay coach Mike Holmgren thinks. Toward the end of Super Bowl XXXII, with the Broncos driving toward the goal line, Holmgren instructed his players to allow Denver to score. He doubted his exhausted defense could keep the Broncos out of the end zone, so he figured that by letting them in right away, Brett Favre would have more time to try for the game-tying score. The strategy did not work, as Green Bay received the ensuing kickoff and Favre was thwarted at midfield.

In the Super Bowl, a coach is only as good as his last decision. Mike Holmgren chose to let the Denver Broncos score in the closing moments of Super Bowl XXXII, but the strategy backfired.

Terrell Davis gives teammates his trademark touchdown salute. The Denver running back gained 157 yards and was named the game's MVP.

Super Bowl XXXIII
January 31, 1999
(1998 Season)
Atlanta Falcons (NFC)
vs. Denver Broncos (AFC)

With nothing left to prove, many of the veterans on Denver's offensive line thought about retiring after their marvelous victory over the Packers in Super Bowl XXXII. When John Elway decided to come back and play one more season, however, they had a change of heart. The old gang came together for one last shot at glory. Denver's opponent, the Atlanta Falcons, was the surprise team of the season. With the vast majority of NFL fans rooting for the Broncos, the "Dirty Birds" had their work cut out for them.

The Broncos had a terrific year. After they opened the season with 13 straight wins, there was talk of a perfect season—something that had never been accomplished since the league switched to a 16-game schedule. A loss to the Giants in December ended this dream, but it turned out to be a blessing in disguise. It gave Mike Shanahan the opportunity to rest his key players for the playoffs. One man who did not rest was Terrell Davis, who became only the fourth runner in history to gain more than 2,000 yards in a season. Elway, meanwhile, was simply fantastic. He threw for nearly 3,000 yards and finished with the AFC's second-best quarterback rating. In all, the Broncos scored 501 points, while their defense allowed only 309.

The Falcons, in their second season under coach Dan Reeves, started the year hoping to achieve a winning record for the first time since 1995. Quarterback Chris Chandler and running back Jamal Anderson had

And Denver's little-noticed, lowly regarded offensive line had won the war in the trenches—which was perhaps the most surprising victory of all.

Broncos 31
Packers 24
Best Player: Terrell Davis

quietly put together solid numbers in 1997. In 1998 they had career years. The addition of receiver Tony Martin was the key. He gave Chandler a third option and made defenses think twice before ganging up on Anderson or star wideout Terence Mathis. The Atlanta defense was good, too. Veterans Cornelius Bennett, Jesse Tuggle, Ray Buchanan, and Eugene Robinson provided leadership and made big plays. A respectable 5-2 start was followed by nine consecutive wins to complete the regular season. Then the Falcons upset the 49ers and powerhouse Vikings in the playoffs to reach the Super Bowl.

For Elway, this game was extra special. It was to be his last as a pro, and it would be played against a coach he knew well. Reeves and Elway had reached the Super Bowl three times together between 1987 and 1990, and they squabbled over strategy before Reeves left in 1993. Now they would meet again—with Elway looking to become the first AFC quarterback since Terry Bradshaw to win back-to-back Super Bowls. Reeves was no less of a story heading into the big game. Miraculously, he was coaching again just a few weeks after undergoing emergency heart surgery. Mike Shanahan also figured in the game's rich story. In 1991 he had been fired by Reeves in Denver, and it still bugged him. Like Elway, Shanahan was motivated to beat his old boss.

The Falcons got off to a surprising start when Morten Anderson booted a 32-yard field goal early in the first quarter. The Broncos went up 7-3 on their next possession, when Elway took the team down the field for the game's first touchdown. After connecting with Rod Smith on a key 41-yard pass play, Elway handed off to full-

back Howard Griffith, who bulled his way across the goal line.

The next surprise came in the second quarter, when the Falcons elected to go for a risky fourth-down play. Anderson got the ball but was swarmed an instant later for no gain. The Broncos took over and moved across midfield to set up a Jason Elam field goal, which made the score 10-3.

Atlanta penetrated deep into Denver territory and appeared poised to even up the score. Then Anderson missed a short kick, which sent shock waves through the Falcon bench. Moments later, Elway took advantage of the situation by sending Rod Smith deep. He hit the wide receiver with a bomb that was good for an 80-yard touchdown and a 17-3 advantage. The Falcons did get their second field goal late in the second quarter, when Anderson chipped a 28-yarder through the uprights to cut Denver's lead to 17-6.

Coach Shanahan was pleased with the Broncos' performance and told them so at halftime. Davis had missed much of the first half with a migraine attack, but his teammates had picked up the slack. Elway was getting great protection and throwing well, and the Denver defense was not making any mistakes. In the Atlanta locker room, Reeves was discussing the very same topics. The defense, he said, would need to do a better job pressuring Elway; the offense would have to make something happen to shake Denver's confidence.

Although Atlanta failed to score in the third quarter, Reeves was pleased with what he saw. Elway could not get into the end zone, and Elam missed two field-goal attempts. The score remained 17-6, and now the Falcons seemed to have the momentum.

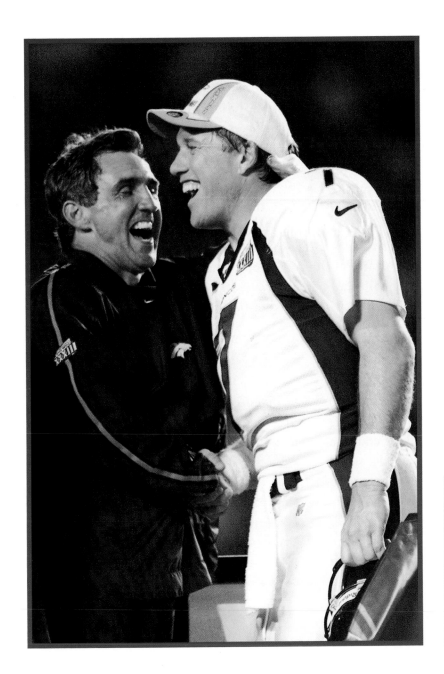

Coach Mike Shanahan and quarterback John Elway celebrate their second NFL championship in a row. Elway retired after this game.

Early in the fourth quarter, Atlanta moved deep into Denver territory. Few in the crowd doubted that the Falcons would score. Cornerback Darrien Gordon had other ideas. When he saw a Chandler pass glance off the fingers of its intended target, he shifted direction, caught the ball, and began to make his way toward the opposite end zone. By the time the Falcons caught up to Gordon, he had

reached the 24-yard line. From there it took Elway just five plays to reach the end zone.

Down 24-6, Chandler was forced to take chances. He went to the air in an attempt to close the deficit quickly, but once again Gordon was there for the interception. A few minutes later, Elway took the ball in himself to extend Denver's lead to 31-6.

A 94-yard touchdown return by Tim

FOND FAREWELL

The dream of every athlete is to go out a winner. John Elway's dream was to go out a multiple winner. Only a handful of stars have accomplished this feat, and only a few of them did so on their own terms. Hockey goalie Ken Dryden hung up his skates after winning four consecutive Stanley Cups. Boxer Rocky Marciano left the ring as history's only undefeated heavyweight. Michael Jordan did it with the Chicago Bulls—twice!—before "unretiring" at the start of the 2001–2002 NBA season.

And then there is Elway, who was good enough in his final season to be selected for the Pro Bowl. His choice as one of the AFC's top passers was not a sentimental one. Besides leading the Broncos to a 14-2 season, he threw for 22 touchdowns and compiled a quarterback rating of 93.0—the best of his entire career!

Dwight gave Atlanta fans something to cheer about, but by then the game's outcome was all but decided. Elam added a field goal late in the quarter to make it 34-13; then Chandler and Mathis hooked up for a short touchdown. The game ended 34-19.

Reeves, who had coached Denver to Super Bowl losses in 1987, 1988, and 1990, praised his team's effort. Perhaps he sensed that this might be his last trip to football's ultimate contest. Elway, who officially retired a few months later, got to do what only a handful of sports stars have ever done: He went out on top, a back-to-back champion.

Broncos 34
Falcons 19
Best Player: John Elway

CHAPTER 5

2000 AND BEYOND

Super Bowl XXXIV
**January 30, 2000
(1999 Season)
St. Louis Rams (NFC)
vs. Tennessee Titans (AFC)**

Football fans love to watch a colorful team. They enjoy rooting for oddballs and renegades and feel a special bond with players plucked off the junk pile. They also like it when an underdog team bites its "master" in the rear end. Unfortunately, teams like this rarely reach the Super Bowl. Usually, they run into an opponent with better coaching and overwhelming talent. In Super Bowl XXXIV, this was not the case. Both teams—the Rams and the Titans—were among the most intriguing franchises of modern times.

The Rams came into existence during the Great Depression. They suspended play during World War II, then abandoned the city of their birth (Cleveland) after winning the NFL championship in 1946. As the Los Angeles Rams, they won it all in 1951, then reached just one more championship game before leaving L.A. for St. Louis 44 years later. Their first four seasons in their new home produced a meager 22 wins.

Then, in 1999, a former grocery-store clerk named Kurt Warner was thrust into the starting quarterback role, and suddenly the Rams' offense was unstoppable. A star in the lightly regarded Arena Football League, Warner brought the indoor game's fast reads and quick throws to the NFL, and no one could figure out how to stop him. Warner worked his magic with four swift receivers and Marshall Faulk, the most versatile back in the game. The St. Louis defense had just the right mix of veterans and youngsters to keep opponents in check and keep the record-setting offense on the field.

The Titans began life in 1960 as the Houston Oilers, one of the original franchises in the American Football League. Their owner, Bud Adams, was one of the millionaires who helped keep the league afloat in its early years. Long before most football fans knew or cared, the Oilers were the class of the AFL. They won big and won small—and they won it all in 1961 and 1962. Some of the game's most colorful personalities passed through Houston over the next three and a half decades. Then, in 1998, Adams moved the team to Tennessee when the city of Houston balked at the idea of building a new stadium. With a core of talented young players like quarterback Steve McNair and running back Eddie

Kevin Dyson of the Titans strains to get the ball over the goal line on the heart-stopping final play of Super Bowl XXXIV.

middle. The key was to "look" linebacker Mike Jones away from Dyson, so that Dyson could catch the ball around the 5-yard line and reach the goal line untouched. Jones followed McNair's eyes and began to lean to his left, but the veteran sensed something was fishy when he saw Dyson suddenly veer in front of him. He held his ground and then moved in for the tackle when Dyson caught McNair's pass. He wrapped himself around Dyson's legs as the receiver lunged for the end zone and brought him down a couple of yards short as time ran out.

The first Super Bowl of the twenty-first century could very well go down in history as the most exciting one ever played. From start to finish, it had fans on the edge of their seats. There were moments of incredible tension; there were heroic feats; and the game was decided by superstars making super plays. And it literally could not have been any closer.

Warner faded back to pass, only to see the monstrous Kearse knife through his pass protection and lunge for him. The rookie barely missed blocking Warner's desperation pass before slamming him to the turf. Downfield, as he sprinted along the right sideline, Isaac Bruce saw that Warner's pass was slightly underthrown. He shifted speed and direction ever so slightly and settled under the pass. Then he shook a trio of defenders and tore down the field for an incredible touchdown.

Ironically, it was the Titans who now had time for one last drive. Behind 23-16, McNair made several great plays to advance the ball to St. Louis's 10-yard line. With one play left—and everyone on the Rams thinking that McNair would throw to the big tight end, Frank Wycheck—the Tennessee quarterback sent Kevin Dyson darting across the

> **Rams 23**
> **Titans 16**
>   Best Player: Kurt Warner

Super Bowl XXXV
January 28, 2001
(2000 Season)
New York Giants (NFC)
vs. Baltimore Ravens (AFC)

For most players, the Super Bowl is a once-in-a-lifetime chance to get noticed by millions. For unknowns, it is an opportunity to make an indelible impression with a great tackle or amazing catch. For players with soiled reputations, there is no better place to change millions of minds. Super Bowl XXXV, between the Ravens and Giants, featured several players seeking a second chance.

Among those looking to do a little image repair were two prominent members of the Ravens. Trent Dilfer, a first-round draft choice by the Tampa Buccaneers in 1994, had practically been run out of town after six so-so years as the team's quarterback. Signed by the Ravens as a backup, he took over the starting job from Tony Banks and ran Baltimore's conservative attack to perfection.

The Ravens were conservative on offense because their defense was so good. Its best player, linebacker Ray Lewis, was also seeking redemption in this game. A year earlier, he had been involved in a fight that ended with two people dead. The killers, friends of Lewis's, escaped with him in his limousine. Although Lewis had been cleared of any involvement in the homicides, many fans thought he belonged behind bars.

For quarterback Kerry Collins of the Giants, just making it to Super Bowl XXXV was a remarkable accomplishment. In 1996, just his second season as a pro, Collins was the talk of football when he led the Carolina Panthers to the NFC championship game. A year later, he had lost his starting job—as well as the support of fans and teammates—and was battling a drinking problem. After being discarded by the lowly New Orleans Saints, Collins was given a final chance with the Giants. He responded with a spectacular season in 2000—making great throws, showing maturity, and becoming the team leader that no one believed he could be. Behind an experienced line, Collins worked wonders with receivers

Amani Toomer and Ike Hilliard, as well as running back Tiki Barber, who caught 70 passes and ran for more than 1,000 yards.

The Ravens had a couple of offensive standouts, too. Tight end Shannon Sharpe had been one of John Elway's favorite receivers during his glory years in Denver. Now he was Dilfer's go-to guy. A pair of players named Lewis were also huge contributors. Jamal Lewis was an accomplished running back, while Jermaine Lewis was a game-breaking return man. They would test the New York defense, which, like Baltimore's, could (and often did) dominate games.

Believing Baltimore would try to establish its running game early, the Giants bunched their defenders close to the line. Dilfer surprised them by going to the air. On three plays in the first quarter alone, he picked on New York's defensive superstar, Jason Sehorn. One of his passes connected with receiver Brandon Stokely, who scored a 38-yard touchdown.

Meanwhile, the New York offense was sputtering. Only twice in the first half did the Giants cross midfield. Their best scoring chance disappeared when Collins was picked off at the goal line by Chris McAlister.

In the second quarter, Dilfer burned Dave Thomas with a long pass to Qadry Ismail. The play went for 44 yards and set up the game's second score, a 47-yard field goal by Matt Stover with less than 2 minutes to play.

In the locker room, the Giants took comfort in their defensive effort. The offense was in trouble, however. On many plays that had succeeded during the regular season and the playoffs, the Giants found a flock of Raven tacklers waiting for them. On several throws, Collins had looked confused and unsure of himself. The Ravens identified this weakness in Collins and planned even more ways to throw him off his game. He was over his head against their defense, and in the second half they planned to press this advantage.

With less than 4 minutes to go in the third quarter and the score still 10-0, cornerback Duane Starks was the first to make Collins pay. In game films he had noticed that Collins had a slight hop in his dropback when he threw quick passes to his right. Starks lined up well off of Toomer and lured Collins into thinking this area was open. As Collins dropped back, Starks spotted the hop and ran immediately to the area where he knew the pass was headed. He intercepted the ball and ran 49 yards for a touchdown.

The Giants got the points back immediately when Ron Dixon, an unknown rookie who had played for three different colleges, fielded Stover's kickoff and raced

Duane Starks heads for the end zone after intercepting a Kerry Collins pass. The Baltimore defense was simply too much for the Giants.

WHEN THE CHEERING STOPPED

For Ray Lewis, Trent Dilfer, and Kerry Collins—the players seeking to boost their fortunes in Super Bowl XXXV—this one-sided contest had mixed results. Lewis was the game's MVP, and his performance in the face of so much criticism probably won him a few more fans. His sins were hardly forgiven, however. He was not invited to yell, "I'm going to Disney World!" as the game's past stars had been. And when the Ravens were featured on a commemorative Wheaties cereal package, Lewis's image was left off the box.

Dilfer, who finally showed he could win it all, was dumped by the Ravens after the season and ended up as a second-stringer for the Seattle Seahawks. Although he had to prove himself all over again, at least he was doing so with a championship ring on his finger.

Collins, who tied a record by throwing four interceptions in the loss to the Ravens, actually came out the big "winner." He carried himself with grace and courage in a humiliating defeat and earned back much of the respect he had lost during his career. Though disappointed, Giant fans were pleased to have a solid quarterback on the team—for the first time in nearly a decade.

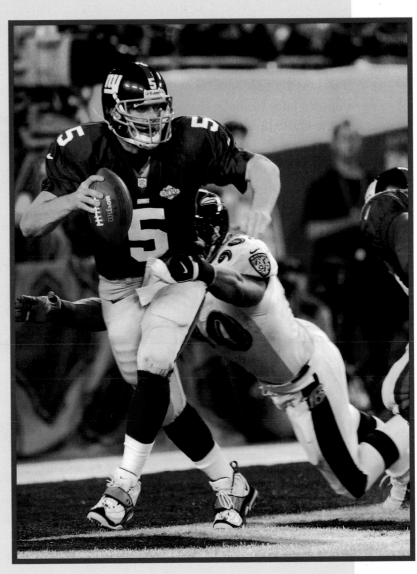

Sometimes winners are found in the losing locker room. Kerry Collins played poorly in Super Bowl XXXV but distinguished himself as a class act in the face of defeat.

97 yards for a touchdown. Prior to kickoff, many believed the game would be decided by defensive backs and special teams. Suddenly, these people were looking pretty smart. They looked like geniuses moments later, when Jermaine Lewis took the Giants' kickoff 84 yards for a touchdown to make it 24-7.

Forced to use their passing attack, the Giants played right into the hands of the Baltimore defense. Time and again, Collins's throws were batted down or failed to produce first downs. In the entire second half, the Giants never entered Raven territory! It was a complete wipeout.

The Ravens added a touchdown 6 minutes into the final quarter and a field goal 3 minutes later to make the final score 34-7. In the entire postseason, the Ravens had allowed just one offensive touchdown and three field goals. In this game, they allowed none. Not since the 1972 Dolphins had a defensive unit so utterly dominated a Super Bowl.

Ravens 34
Giants 7
   Best Player: Ray Lewis

Super Bowl XXXVI
February 3, 2002
(2001 Season)
St. Louis Rams (NFC) vs.
New England Patriots (AFC)

Not since the third Super Bowl, when the Colts were installed as three-touchdown favorites over the Jets, had two teams appeared so mismatched heading into the big game. Simply put, no one seemed sure what

the New England Patriots had, while the St. Louis Rams seemed to have it all. Man for man, the Rams were better at virtually every position.

St. Louis quarterback Kurt Warner was now established as one of the best passers in history. His receiving corps, which featured Isaac Bruce and Torry Holt, was deep and talented. Running back Marshall Faulk was the best all-around player in football. And under offensive-minded head coach Mike Martz, the Rams were firing on all cylinders. The St. Louis defense, the team's lone weakness in years past, had been beefed up with the additions of several key veterans,

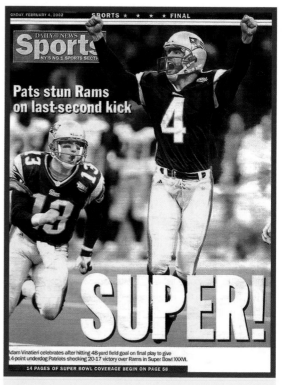

Pats stun Rams on last-second kick

Adam Vinatieri celebrates after hitting 48-yard field goal on final play to give 14-point underdog Patriots shocking 20-17 victory over Rams in Super Bowl XXXVI.

14 PAGES OF SUPER BOWL COVERAGE BEGIN ON PAGE 58

Tom Brady (#13) and Adam Vinatieri (#4) made headlines by beating the heavily favored St. Louis Rams in Super Bowl XXXVI.

most notably cornerback Aeneas Williams. After a carefree 14-2 regular season, the Rams demolished Green Bay and then staved off a desperate rally by the Eagles to make it to the Super Bowl.

The Patriots' path was full of twists and turns. The team began the year 0-2, then lost its star quarterback, Drew Bledsoe, to injury. New England fans, sensing the team would go only as far as Bledsoe could take it, prepared for the worst. But the Pats surprised everyone by rallying around second-year quarterback Tom Brady and winning the AFC East. Despite the fact he was just 24, Brady proved to be one of the best-prepared backups in the league. He limited his mistakes, exploited opponents' weaknesses, and did just enough to win 11 of the team's final 14 games. Brady was aided by a surprisingly good offensive line, a surprising return to form of former 1,000-yard rusher Antowain Smith, and the surprising development of Troy Brown into an electrifying receiver and special teams star. Under coach Bill Belichick, the New England defense hit hard and mastered a tricky system that wore other teams down and forced turnovers.

New England had chemistry, which meant it had a chance. Belichick's game plan was to keep crashing into the Rams until their offense got out of sync, then wait for an opportunity to strike. From the opening kickoff, the Patriots executed this plan to perfection. Whenever a St. Louis receiver came near a ball, he got leveled. Whenever Faulk carried the ball, the Pats put an extra body on him to bring him down. Warner, who is as tough as they come, took a hit early in the game and injured the thumb on his throwing hand. It was not enough to make him leave the game, but it made each pass a painful one. In the second quarter, defensive back Ty Law stepped in front of a wobbly Warner delivery and intercepted the ball. He ran 47 yards for a touchdown to give New England a 7-3 lead. Just before halftime, Brady hit David Patten in the end zone to make it 14-3.

Belichick warned his players to be ready for a wild second half. Martz, confident the Rams would come back, told them to remain clam and do what they did best. The third quarter was a war, with New England extending its lead to 17-3 on an Adam Vinatieri field goal. The fourth quarter saw the St. Louis comeback everyone was expecting. Warner drove his team to the two-yard line, then scored on a run to make the score 17-10. Minutes later, he tied the score with a lovely 26-yard touchdown throw to Ricky Proehl. With 90 seconds left, everyone braced for the first overtime in Super Bowl history.

Belichick had other ideas. He told Brady to go for a score. The young man who had thrown all of three passes the season before set his jaw, eyed the St. Louis defense, and began zipping short passes. Starting from his own 17-yard line with no timeouts, Brady maneuvered the team across midfield like his childhood hero, Joe Montana. With seven seconds left, the Patriots stopped the clock on the 31-yard line. Vinatieri, who had made several clutch kicks during New England's remarkable season, made one last one to give the Pats a 20-17 upset victory.

Patriots 20
Rams 17
    Best Player: Tom Brady

TOM TERRIFIC

Although it was the New England defense that deserved credit for a perfectly played game, Tom Brady was named the MVP of Super Bowl XXXVI. He defied the experts and played with poise and professionalism, despite dire predictions and overwhelming odds. To those who knew Brady, however, his MVP performance was hardly a surprise.

"Be prepared" may be the Boy Scout motto, but it also was a saying Brady had learned to take to heart. At every stop on his road to the Super Bowl—beginning in middle school—he was the backup quarterback who had to patiently wait his turn. Even when Brady knew he was better than the starter, he kept his mouth shut, learned the playbook, worked like a dog in practice, and was 100 percent ready when the call came. And at every level he distinguished himself as a winner and a star.

Is Brady a "flash in the pan," or was his Super Bowl victory a preview of things to come? The Patriots answered that question loudly and clearly the following spring, when longtime starter Drew Bledsoe was shipped to the Buffalo Bills and Brady was anointed the starter.

NFL teams spend millions of dollars looking for that one player with good abilities, a great heart, and the kind of leadership skills that bring out the best in his teammates. In Brady, a lowly sixth-round draft pick, the Patriots found one right under their noses. And they weren't about to let him get away.

Quarterback Tom Brady and head coach Bill Belichick (Right) celebrate their win over the St. Louis Rams on February 3, 2002 in Super Bowl XXXVI.

SUPER BOWL CHAMPIONS

Game	Date	
XXXVI	Feb. 3, 2002	New England 20, St. Louis 17
XXXV	Jan. 28, 2001	Baltimore 34, N.Y. Giants 7
XXXIV	Jan. 30, 2000	St. Louis 23, Tennessee 16
XXXIII	Jan. 31, 1999	Denver 34, Atlanta 19
XXXII	Jan. 25, 1998	Denver 31, Green Bay 24
XXXI	Jan. 26, 1997	Green Bay 35, New England 21
XXX	Jan. 28, 1996	Dallas 27, Pittsburgh 17
XXIX	Jan. 29, 1995	San Francisco 49, San Diego 26
XXVIII	Jan. 30, 1994	Dallas 30, Buffalo 13
XXVII	Jan. 31, 1993	Dallas 52, Buffalo 17
XXVI	Jan. 26, 1992	Washington 37, Buffalo 24
XXV	Jan. 27, 1991	N.Y. Giants 20, Buffalo 19
XXIV	Jan. 28, 1990	San Francisco 55, Denver 10
XXIII	Jan. 22, 1989	San Francisco 20, Cincinnati 16
XXII	Jan. 31, 1988	Washington 42, Denver 10
XXI	Jan. 25, 1987	N.Y. Giants 39, Denver 20
XX	Jan. 26, 1986	Chicago 46, New England 10
XIX	Jan. 20, 1985	San Francisco 38, Miami 16
XVIII	Jan. 22, 1984	L.A. Raiders 38, Washington 9
XVII	Jan. 30, 1983	Washington 27, Miami 17
XVI	Jan. 24, 1982	San Francisco 26, Cincinnati 21
XV	Jan. 25, 1981	Oakland 27, Philadelphia 10
XIV	Jan. 20, 1980	Pittsburgh 31, L.A. Rams 19
XIII	Jan. 21, 1979	Pittsburgh 35, Dallas 31
XII	Jan. 15, 1978	Dallas 27, Denver 10
XI	Jan. 9, 1977	Oakland 32, Minnesota 14
X	Jan. 18, 1976	Pittsburgh 21, Dallas 17
IX	Jan. 12, 1975	Pittsburgh 16, Minnesota 6
VIII	Jan. 13, 1974	Miami 24, Minnesota 7
VII	Jan. 14, 1973	Miami 14, Washington 7
VI	Jan. 16, 1972	Dallas 24, Miami 3
V	Jan. 17, 1971	Baltimore 16, Dallas 13
IV	Jan. 11, 1970	Kansas City 23, Minnesota 7
III	Jan. 12, 1969	N.Y. Jets 16, Baltimore 7
II	Jan. 14, 1968	Green Bay 33, Oakland 14
I	Jan. 15, 1967	Green Bay 35, Kansas City 10

NFC CHAMPIONSHIP GAMES

(Home Team in Capital Letters)

2001	ST. LOUIS 29, Philadelphia 24
2000	NY GIANTS 41, Minnesota 0
1999	ST. LOUIS 11, Tampa Bay 6
1998	Atlanta 30, MINNESOTA 27 (OT)
1997	Green Bay 23, SAN FRANCISCO 10
1996	GREEN BAY 30, Carolina 13
1995	DALLAS 38, Green Bay 27
1994	SAN FRANCISCO 38, Dallas 28
1993	DALLAS 38, San Francisco 21
1992	Dallas 30, SAN FRANCISCO 20
1991	WASHINGTON 41, Detroit 10
1990	NY Giants 15, SAN FRANCISCO 13
1989	SAN FRANCISCO 30, LA Rams 3
1988	San Francisco 28, CHICAGO BEARS 3
1987	WASHINGTON 17, Minnesota 10
1986	NY GIANTS 17, Washington 0
1985	CHICAGO BEARS 24, LA Rams 0
1984	SAN FRANCISCO 23, Chicago Bears 0
1983	WASHINGTON 24, San Francisco 21
1982	WASHINGTON 31, Dallas 17
1981	SAN FRANCISCO 28, Dallas 27
1980	PHILADELPHIA 20, Dallas 7
1979	LA Rams 9, TAMPA BAY 0
1978	Dallas 28, LA RAMS 0
1977	DALLAS 23, Minnesota 6
1976	MINNESOTA 24, LA Rams 13
1975	Dallas 37, LA RAMS 7
1974	MINNESOTA 14, LA Rams 10
1973	Minnesota 27, DALLAS 10
1972	WASHINGTON 26, Dallas 3
1971	DALLAS 14, San Francisco 3
1970	Dallas 17, SAN FRANCISCO 10

NFL CHAMPIONSHIP GAMES

(Home Team in Capital Letters)

1969	MINNESOTA 27, Cleveland 7
1968	Baltimore 34, CLEVELAND 0
1967	GREEN BAY 21, Dallas 17
1966	Green Bay 34, DALLAS 27
1965	GREEN BAY 23, Cleveland 12
1964	CLEVELAND 27, Baltimore 0

NFL CHAMPIONSHIP GAMES (continued)

1963	CHICAGO BEARS 14, NY Giants 10
1962	Green Bay 16, NY GIANTS 7
1961	GREEN BAY 37, NY Giants 0
1960	PHILADELPHIA 17, Green Bay 13
1959	BALTIMORE 31, NY Giants 16
1958	Baltimore 23, NY GIANTS 17 (OT)
1957	DETROIT 59, Cleveland 14
1956	NY GIANTS 47, Chicago Bears 7
1955	Cleveland 38, LA RAMS 14
1954	CLEVELAND 56, Detroit 10
1953	DETROIT 17, Cleveland 16
1952	Detroit 17, CLEVELAND 7
1951	LA RAMS 24, Cleveland 17
1950	CLEVELAND 30, LA Rams 28
1949	Philadelphia 14, LA RAMS 0
1948	PHILADELPHIA 7, Chicago Cardinals 0
1947	CHICAGO CARDINALS 28, Philadelphia 21
1946	Chicago Bears 24, NY GIANTS 14
1945	CLEVELAND 15, Washington 14
1944	Green Bay 14, NY GIANTS 7
1943	CHICAGO BEARS 41, Washington 21
1942	WASHINGTON 14, Chicago Bears 6
1941	CHICAGO BEARS 37, NY Giants 9
1940	Chicago Bears 73, WASHINGTON 0
1939	GREEN BAY 27, NY Giants 0
1938	NY GIANTS 23, Green Bay 17
1937	Washington 28, CHICAGO BEARS 21
1936	Green Bay 21, BOSTON 6
1935	DETROIT 26, NY Giants 7
1934	NY GIANTS 30, Chicago 13
1933	CHICAGO BEARS 23, NY Giants 21
1932	CHICAGO BEARS 9, Portsmouth 0

AFC CHAMPIONSHIP GAMES

	(Home Team in Capital Letters)
2001	New England 24, PITTSBURGH 17
2000	Baltimore 16, OAKLAND 3
1999	Tennessee 33, JACKSONVILLE 14
1998	DENVER 23, NY Jets 10
1997	Denver 24, PITTSBURGH 21
1996	NEW ENGLAND 20, Jacksonville 6
1995	PITTSBURGH 20, Indianapolis 16

AFC CHAMPIONSHIP GAMES (continued)

1994	San Diego 17, PITTSBURGH 13
1993	BUFFALO 30, Kansas City 13
1992	Buffalo 29, MIAMI 10
1991	BUFFALO 10, Denver 7
1990	BUFFALO 51, LA Raiders 3
1989	DENVER 37, Cleveland 21
1988	CINCINNATI 21, Buffalo 10
1987	DENVER 38, Cleveland 33
1986	Denver 23, CLEVELAND 20 (OT)
1985	New England 31, MIAMI 14
1984	MIAMI 45, Pittsburgh 28
1983	LA RAIDERS 30, Seattle 14
1982	MIAMI 14, NY Jets 0
1981	CINCINNATI 27, San Diego 7
1980	Oakland 34, SAN DIEGO 27
1979	PITTSBURGH 27, Houston 13
1978	PITTSBURGH 34, Houston 5
1977	DENVER 20, Oakland 17
1976	OAKLAND 24, Pittsburgh 7
1975	PITTSBURGH 16, Oakland 10
1974	PITTSBURGH 24, Oakland 13
1973	MIAMI 27, Oakland 10
1972	Miami 21, PITTSBURGH 17
1971	MIAMI 21, Baltimore 0
1970	BALTIMORE 27, Oakland 17

AFL CHAMPIONSHIP GAMES

	(Home Team in Capital Letters)
1969	Kansas City 17, OAKLAND 7
1968	NY JETS 27, Oakland 23
1967	OAKLAND 40, Houston 7
1966	Kansas City 31, BUFFALO 7
1965	Buffalo 23, SAN DIEGO 0
1964	BUFFALO 20, San Diego 7
1963	SAN DIEGO 51, Boston 10
1962	Dallas Texans 20, HOUSTON 17
1961	Houston 10, SAN DIEGO 3
1960	HOUSTON 24, LA Chargers 16

For More Information

Some good books on football

Allen, George, with Ben Olan. *Pro Football's 100 Greatest Players*. Indianapolis, Indiana: Bobbs-Merrill, 1982.

Carroll, Bob. *When the Grass Was Real*. New York: Simon & Schuster, 1993.

Carroll, Bob, Michael Gershman, David Neft, and John Thorn. *Total Football: The Official Encyclopedia of the National Football*. New York: HarperCollins, 1997.

Korch, Rick. *The Truly Great*. Dallas, Texas: Taylor Publishing, 1993.

Kramer, Jerry. *Distant Replay*. New York: GP Putnam's Sons, 1985.

Lazenby, Roland. *The Super Bowl*. New York: Gallery Books, 1988.

Maraniss, David. *When Pride Still Mattered*. New York: Simon & Schuster, 1999.

Montana, Joe, with Dick Schaap. *Montana*. Atlanta, Georgia: Turner Publishing, 1995.

Murphy, Austin. *The Super Bowl*. New York: Time Inc. Home Entertainment, 1998.

Neft, David, Richard Cohen, and Rick Korch. *The Sports Encyclopedia: Pro Football*. New York: St. Martin's Press, 2002.

Shula, Don, with Lou Sahadi. *The Winning Edge*. New York: E.P. Dutton & Co., 1973.

St. John, Bob. *TEX! The Man Who Built the Dallas Cowboys*. Englewood Cliffs, New Jersey: Prentice Hall, 1988.

Index

Page numbers in *italics* indicate illustrations.

About the Author

Mark Stewart ranks among the busiest sportswriters today. He has produced hundreds of profiles on athletes past and present and has authored more than 80 books, including all 10 titles in **The Watts History of Sports.** A graduate of Duke University, Stewart is currently president of Team Stewart, Inc., a sports information and resource company in New Jersey.